Credits

 KU-076-793

This Resource Guide, and the software described in it, is furnished under an end user License Agreement, which is included with the product. The agreement specifies the permitted and prohibited uses.

Trademarks

Copyrights

Introduction

Welcome to the PagePlus X7 Resource Guide.

This Resource Guide covers the best techniques for using the fundamental tools in PagePlus, from beginner- to advanced-level, and provides creative inspiration for producing your publications.

1: PagePlus Features

The tutorials in this chapter help you work with the tools and content available in PagePlus X7. You'll learn how to use these fundamental tools and professional features to create dynamic and eye-catching publications.

2: Projects

In this chapter, we've gathered together a collection of popular projects. Each project explores a range of tools and features, and contains a wealth of information and techniques for using PagePlus.

3: Creative Showcase

Be inspired by the work in this chapter! We showcase a few Pro Design Templates and theme layouts alongside examples created using assets and object styles. Instructions on accessing these templates and theme layouts are also included.

Working with tutorials

Throughout the Resource Guide, you'll be prompted to access resource files from the **Assets** tab within PagePlus (located to the left of your workspace). These files have been provided to get you started or to help focus on a key learning point. Details for accessing these files are provided within the tutorial.

Useful icons

Here is a quick guide to the icons you'll find useful along the way.

 Don't forget to save your work! We'll remind you along the way with these helpful save points.

 These give you an estimate of how long a tutorial will take to complete.

 For guidance, tutorials are graded between 1 (beginner) - 5 (advanced).

 This is a note. Notes provide useful information about the program or a particular technique.

 This is a tip. Our tips provide information that will help you with your projects.

 This is a warning! We don't want to make you panic but when you see this icon, you need to pay attention to the steps as they will be particularly important.

Further Resources

- **Online video tutorials**

  These videos guide you through a range of techniques for using the tools available in PagePlus.

  Available from the PagePlus Startup Assistant's **Learn** section.

- **Comprehensive PagePlus Help**

  The PagePlus Help provides information and instructions on using all the tools, features, and settings within PagePlus.

  Available via the **Help** menu (or press the **F1** key).

Exploring PagePlus X7

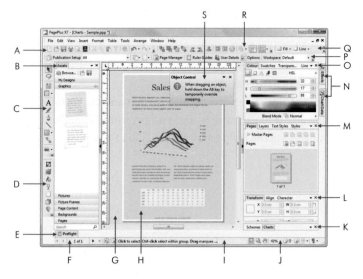

(**A**) Standard toolbar, (**B**) Assets tab, (**C**) Tools toolbar, (**D**) Attributes toolbar, (**E**) Preflight tab (auto hidden), (**F**) Page Navigation tools, (**G**) Pasteboard, (**H**) Page area, (**I**) Hintline toolbar, (**J**) View tools, (**K**) Schemes & Charts tabs (collapsed), (**L**) Transform, Align & Character tabs, (**M**) Pages, Layers, Text Styles & Styles tabs, (**N**) Effects & Chart Data tabs (auto hidden) (**O**) Colour, Swatches, Transparency & Line tabs, (**P**) Context toolbar, (**Q**) Colours toolbar, (**R**) Arrange toolbar, (**S**) Smart Hints.

The PagePlus workspace

The PagePlus workspace consists of:

- Your **page** area (H), for placing text, graphics, and other objects that will appear in the final publication.

- The **pasteboard** area (G), for storing page elements before being positioned on the page area. Objects on the pasteboard are accessible from any page. (The pasteboard and any objects on it will not appear when your publication is published.)

- The **Assets** tab (B), for storing and enabling quick access to content such as graphics, pictures, frames, backgrounds, and page layouts.

- A range of other **tabs**, to help you organize your workflow and modify your publication design.

  Tab groups can be hidden or displayed by clicking the arrows on the left and right of the workspace.

- Horizontal and vertical **toolbars**, used to access PagePlus commands and tools.

Move the mouse pointer around the screen and you'll see popup **tooltips** that identify toolbar buttons and flyouts.

Right-click any object or page region to bring up a **context menu** of functions.

As you work in PagePlus, certain actions will trigger Smart Hints to appear on the workspace. Search *Smart Hints* in PagePlus Help for more information.

Table of Contents

PagePlus Features **1**

Artistic text 3

Pictures... 13

Frame text 27

Assets 45

Logos... 67

Master pages 77

Tables.. 93

Charts 107

Colour schemes.. 129

Object styles... 141

Projects **153**

Page numbering.. 155

Text styles... 169

Creating an eBook 181

Creative Showcase **199**

Pro Templates 201

Theme Layouts... 205

Assets and object styles... 209

PagePlus Features

PagePlus is all about creating stunning publications. In this section, we'll explore the fundamental tools within PagePlus which allow you to design using text, pictures, assets, logos, master pages, tables, charts, colour schemes, and object styles.

1

Artistic text

 10 min

Artistic text is standalone text that can be typed directly onto a page. Its unique properties make it especially useful for titles, pull quotes, and other special-purpose text.

By the end of this tutorial you will be able to:

- Add artistic text to the page.

- Apply a gradient fill to text.

- Create text on a path.

- Rotate and reposition artistic text.

- Update user details.

Let's begin...

1. On the **File** menu, click **Startup Assistant**.

2. On the left, click **New Publication**.

3. Click to select **A4** or **Letter** size paper.

   A single, blank page will open in the workspace.

Although we are working with artistic text in this tutorial, many of the methods described below are applicable to both artistic and frame text. The special properties of artistic text allow you to:

- Stretch or squash the text to create a stylistic effect.

- Create shaped text by putting the text on a path.

Creating Artistic text

Now let's create a new artistic text object...

To create artistic text:

1. On the **Tools** toolbar, click the **A** **Artistic Text Tool**.

2. Click anywhere on your page to set a text insertion point.

3. On the context toolbar, from the styles drop-down list, select **Heading**.

4. Type 'COGNAC'.

5. On the **Align** tab:

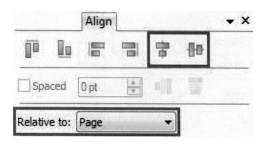

- From the **Relative to** drop-down list, select Page.

- Click ▮▮ **Centre Vertically** and ▮ **Centre Horizontally**.

Your text should now resemble ours...

COGNAC

> We used a preset Text Style to format the artistic text above. Search *Using text styles* in PagePlus Help for more information.
>
> However, you can always set the font, size and text formatting independently using the context toolbar. Search *Setting text properties* and *Using fonts* in PagePlus Help for more information.

Now that our basic title is placed, let's make it a little more interesting by stretching it.

To resize artistic text:

• With the text object still selected, on the **Transform** tab:

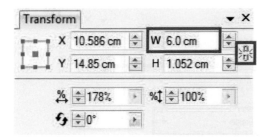

• Ensure ⚏ **Lock Aspect Ratio** is off. (If not, click the button once.)

• Change the Width to **6.0 cm**.

COGNAC

Save now! Click **File** > **Save As** and type a new file name.

Using gradient fills on text

The title already has impact, but we can make it even more powerful by applying a gradient fill.

To apply a gradient fill:

1. Click the border of the text object to select it (the border turns solid).

2. On the **Swatches** tab:

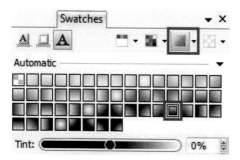

*   From the **Gradient** flyout, select **Automatic**.

*   Click any swatch to apply it to the text.

> The **Automatic** palette sets the gradient based on the colour(s) already applied to your object.

COGNAC

The gradient colour spread works well, but we can make it look even better by matching it with the publication's colour scheme.

To edit a gradient fill to match a publication's colour scheme:

1. Click to select the text object (the border turns solid) and then, on the **Attributes** toolbar, click the ⬥ **Fill Tool**.

    The object's fill path is displayed.

2. On the context toolbar, from the **End Colour** flyout, select **Scheme Colour 2**.

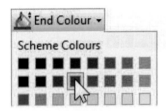

Now our text matches the publication's colour scheme.

COGNAC

See *Colour schemes* on p. 129 for more information regarding scheme colours.

Don't forget to save your work!

Text on a path

To explore some other areas of artistic text, we're going to add the company's web address to the page. For that extra special touch, we'll create it on a curved path.

To place text on a path:

1.　On the **Tools** toolbar, click the **A** **Artistic Text Tool**.

2.　Position the cursor below the title text and centred on the page—dynamic guides will appear to help you.

　　Click to set the text insertion point.

> As you are using the Artistic Text Tool, the text's style is automatically set to Artistic Body.

3.　On the **Insert** menu, select **Information > User Details**.

4.　In the **User Details** dialog, select **(Business) Web Site URL** and click **OK**.

The company URL stored in the **User Details** is inserted on the page.

5. On the context toolbar, in the **Path Text** flyout, select **Path - Wave**.

The path is applied.

The path text looks good, but we can rotate and reposition it to fit our intended design.

 You can reposition and rotate any artistic text objects in the way described below.

 Don't forget to save your work!

To rotate and reposition artistic text:

1. Click the border of the path text object to select it (the border turns solid).

2. Position the cursor over the border's rotation handle and then drag to rotate the path text.

3. Drag the  move button, or the object border, to move the object to curve around the end of the title.

Your design my still contain placeholder user details, so we'll change this next.

To update User Details:

1. On the **Tools** menu, click **Set User Details**.

2. In the **User Details** dialog, on the **Business Sets** tab, type your company's web address in the **Web Site URL** input box and click **Update**.

    These changes will immediately update on your page.

 We updated our User Details for a company called 'Cognac', with a website address 'www.cognac.com'.

That's it! Your artistic text design is now complete.

We hope that you've enjoyed this tutorial. You should now be quite adept at using artistic text. Have fun!

 Don't forget to save your work!

Pictures

10 min

The right pictures can make your publication stand out from the crowd. PagePlus offers a variety of tools and techniques for working with the pictures within your publication.

By the end of this tutorial you will be able to:

- Add pictures to existing frames.

- Add pictures to and use the Assets tab.

- Insert a new frame.

Let's begin...

3.   On the **File** menu, click **Startup Assistant**.

4.   On the left, click **New Publication**.

5.   Click to select **A4** or **Letter** size paper.

A single, blank page will open in the workspace.

For this tutorial, we'll use some of the assets found in the **Tutorials** assets pack installed with PagePlus.

To add tutorial assets to the Assets tab:

1.   On the **Assets** tab, click **Browse** to open the **Asset Browser**.

2.   In the **Pack Files** section, select the **Tutorials** pack.

3.   In the main pane, the assets are categorized by the category they belong to. In the **Pages** category, click pages **1** and **2**. (Page names appear as tooltips.)

The green shows that the asset has been added to the tab.

4.   Click **Close** to exit.

To add a Pages asset to the publication:

1. On the **Assets** tab, the **Pages** category should be displayed (if not, click the **Pages** header).

2. Drag the **1** page thumbnail onto the page.

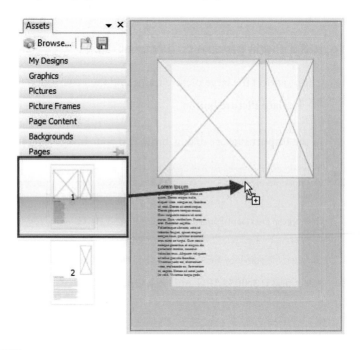

 Save now! Click **File > Save As** and type a new file name.

Adding pictures to an existing frame

This page provides two 'placeholder' picture frames. We'll now look at the different ways in which you can add pictures to the frames.

We'll be using the sample pictures installed with PagePlus. However, you can use your own pictures if you prefer.

To add a single picture to a frame:

1. Click to select the large picture frame and then click the
    Replace Picture button.

2. In the **Import Picture** dialog, browse to your **Images** folder.

In a standard installation, the image files can be accessed from the following location:

C:\Program Files\Serif\PagePlus\X7\Images or
C:\Program Files (x86)\Serif\PagePlus\X7\Images

However, the path may differ if you changed the installation location.

3. Select **060313c0052.JPG** and click **Open**.

The picture is added to the frame and scaled to fit.

When the picture is selected, note that the picture frame toolbar displays in the lower-right corner.

You can use these tools to adjust your picture inside the frame.

To adjust a picture inside a frame:

* To reposition the picture inside the frame, click  **Pan**, and then drag on the picture with the cursor.

* To rotate the picture anti-clockwise, in 90° increments, click **Rotate**.

* To zoom in or out of the picture, click **Zoom In** or **Zoom Out**.

* To replace the picture, click **Replace Picture**, select a new picture, and then click **Open**.

Using the Assets tab

If you're working with lots of pictures, or are not sure which pictures will work best in your publication, you might prefer to add them to the **Assets** tab before adding them to the layout.

PagePlus X7 is supplied with a selection of **Asset packs** each containing pictures, graphics, backgrounds and various other page elements. We'll use some more of the assets found in the **Tutorials** assets pack.

To add tutorial assets to the Assets tab:

1.　On the **Assets** tab, click **Browse** to open the **Asset Browser**.

2.　In the **Pack Files** section, select the **Tutorials** pack.

3.　To display only the pictures, press the **Ctrl** key and then click the **Pictures** category.

4.　Click each of the food related thumbnails.

The green shows that it has been added to the tab.

5.　Click **Close** to exit.

You can also add your own pictures to the **Assets** tab, and even save them as an Asset pack for use in other projects. Search *Using assets* and *Creating custom Asset Packs* in PagePlus Help for more information.

Now that we have imported our pictures, we can add them to the page.

To add a picture to an existing frame:

1. On the **Assets** tab, the **Pictures** category should be displayed (if not, click the **Pictures** header).

2. Drag a picture of your choice onto the empty picture frame.

The picture is cropped to fit the frame boundary.

By using frames for your pictures, it's easy to replace one picture with another, if you decide to change your page design.

To replace a picture in a frame:

● Drag another picture from the **Assets** tab onto the small frame.

The picture adjusts to fit the neatly inside the frame.

 If you have a publication with lots of empty picture frames, you can populate them all in an instance by clicking AutoFlow on the Pictures category of the Assets tab. Search *Adding Pictures* in PagePlus Help for more information.

Inserting a blank picture frame

Now that the first page is complete, let's have a look at another page.
Along the way, we'll show you some more image techniques.

To add a new Page asset:

1. On the **Assets** tab, click the **Pages** category header.

2. Drag the **2** page thumbnail to the right of the current page.

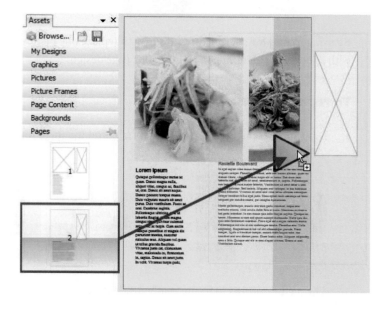

When an arrow appears pointing to the right, release the mouse
button to place the page.

The new page displays automatically.

Now we've added a second page to our publication, we can modify it by adding a new, blank picture frame. We can align this with other objects on the page using dynamic guides.

 Dynamic guides allow you to align new objects to the last three selected page objects.

To use dynamic guides:

1. On the **Arrange** toolbar:

- Ensure  **Snapping** is enabled.

- From the **Snapping** flyout, ensure **Dynamic Guides** is enabled.

2. Click to select the 'Raclette Boulevard' text frame and then click to select the blank picture frame.

Now, we'll create a new picture frame...

To insert a picture frame:

1. On the **Tools** toolbar, on the Picture flyout, click the ⊠ **Rectangular Picture Frame**.

2. Position the cursor near the top of the page. You should see the dynamic guides appear to help you position your picture frame.

3. Drag to begin creating the frame. Release the mouse button when the edges line up with the dynamic guides.

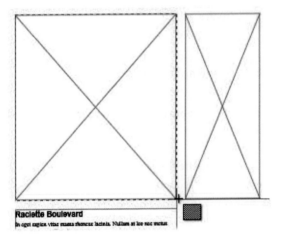

4. Drag the picture of the steak from the **Assets** tab and onto the picture frame.

5. On the picture frame toolbar, click the 🔍 **Zoom In** button a couple of times to zoom into the image, then click the 🖐 **Pan** button to reposition the focus of the picture.

That's it! We've reached the end of this tutorial on pictures. You should now be able to confidently add pictures to your own publications. Why not add a final photo to the last remaining empty frame?

 Don't forget to save your work!

Why not use your saved publication as a starting point for completing the *Frame text* tutorial on p. 27? Have fun!

There's so much more you can do!

Below is an example of what else you can do...

Applying image adjustments

When you select a picture, the context toolbar automatically displays at the top of the workspace.

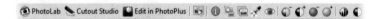

This toolbar provides quick and easy access to key picture-related controls—replace, resize, recolour, and so on—and also lets you apply useful image adjustments, such as red eye removal and brightness and contrast adjustments, with a single click.

PagePlus includes a powerful **PhotoLab** dialog, which you can open by clicking **PhotoLab** on the context toolbar. Search *Applying PhotoLab filters* in PagePlus Help for more information.

Frame text

 25-30 min

This tutorial shows how to create and manipulate frames, frame text, and apply text styles.

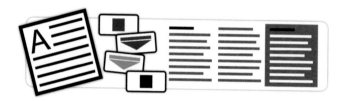

By the end of this tutorial you will be able to:

- Select and edit text.

- Create new text frames.

- Link story text between frames.

- Format and get creative with text frames.

- Apply text styles.

- Create placeholder text.

If you have already completed the *Pictures* tutorial on p. 13, you can use your saved publication for this tutorial.

Let's begin...

1. On the **File** menu, click **Startup Assistant**.

2. On the left, click **New Publication**.

3. Click to select **A4** or **Letter** size paper.

    A single, blank page will open in the workspace.

For this tutorial, we'll use some of the assets found in the **Tutorials** assets pack.

To add tutorial assets to the Assets tab:

1. On the **Assets** tab, click **Browse** to open the **Asset Browser**.

2. In the **Pack Files** section, select the **Tutorials** pack.

3. In the main pane, the assets are categorized by the category they belong to. In the **Pages** category, click pages **1** and **2**. (Page names appear as tooltips.)

The green shows that the asset has been added to the tab.

4. Click **Close** to exit.

To add a Pages asset to the publication:

1. On the **Assets** tab, the **Pages** category should be displayed (if not, click the **Pages** header).

2. Drag the **1** page thumbnail onto the page.

 Save now! Click **File** > **Save As** and type a new file name.

About frame text

PagePlus provides two types of text—**frame text** and **artistic text**. Frame text is placed on the page inside a text frame, and is generally used for general copy, longer passages of text or non-decorative text such as contact details, product information, etc.

Artistic text is most often used for titles and decorative text. For more on artistic text, see *Artistic text* on p. 3.

Frame text has several special properties. It enables you to:

- Flow text between linked frames.

- Wrap text around pictures and shapes.

- Shape the frame to page objects.

Many of the methods described in the following sections, such as selecting and editing text, are applicable to both artistic and frame text.

First, we'll show you how to select, edit, and format text.

To select and edit text:

1. Click on the 'Lorem Ipsum' titled text frame at the bottom-left of the page.

    The Hintline toolbar tells you that this is a text frame.

2. Click to place an insertion point after 'Ipsum' and then drag to the left to select the entire line of text.

3. Type 'Croissant Avenue'.

The title is complete and you've now used one of the methods to select text. Let's move on to look at some of the ways we can edit a text frame.

Linked frames

In PagePlus, you can link multiple text frames. This allows the text to flow from one frame to another automatically. Click inside the text frame once again.

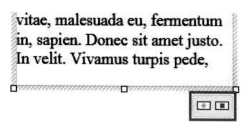

Notice that it shows two different buttons,  **AutoFlow** and **Overflow**. These show that the frame contains more story text than can be displayed in the frame. We can fix this by creating new text frames for the text to flow into.

We can align these new text frames with other objects on the page using dynamic guides.

Dynamic guides allow you to align new objects to the last three selected page objects.

To use dynamic guides:

1. On the **Arrange** toolbar:

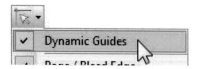

*   Ensure **Snapping** is enabled.

*   From the **Snapping** flyout, ensure **Dynamic Guides** is enabled.

2.   Click to select the left picture frame and then click to select the text frame.

Now, we'll create a new text frame and link the story text.

To create a new text frame:

1.   On the **Tools** toolbar, click ▣ **Standard Text Frame**.

2.   Move the cursor in line with the top of the first frame and slightly to the right.

A red dynamic guide appears when the cursor is in line.

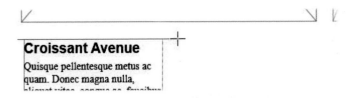

3.   Drag across and down the page until the next set of dynamic guides appear on the right (to align with the picture frame) and the bottom (to align with the text frame).

4.   The frame is created when you release the mouse button.

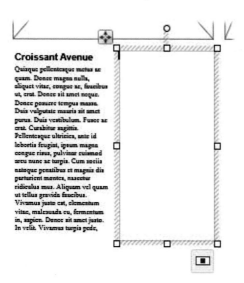

Now that we have an empty frame, we can link this frame to the text frame that contains the overflow text.

To link existing text frames:

1.   Click inside the left text frame containing the text.

     The ⊞ **AutoFlow** and ▣ **Overflow** buttons are displayed.

2.   Click the ▣ **Overflow** button.

     The cursor will change to ▦.

3. Hover over the new text frame and click once when the edges glow.

The text flows into the new frame, which is now linked to the first frame.

As you can see, the 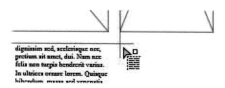 **AutoFlow** and **Overflow** buttons are still available, meaning that the linked frames still contain additional text.

Click inside the first frame. Notice that a **Continued (Overflow)** button is displayed. This indicates that the frame is now linked, but that the last frame in the sequence still contains overflow text. Let's fix this now.

To create a linked text frame:

1. Click to select the right picture frame (for alignment purposes) and then click inside the second text frame so that the **AutoFlow** and **Overflow** buttons are displayed.

2. Click the **Overflow** button.

3. Move the pointer in line with the top of the second frame and the left edge of the right picture frame.

    A set of dynamic guides appear when the pointer is correctly positioned.

4. Drag across and down the page until a page margin appears on the right and a dynamic guide at the bottom.

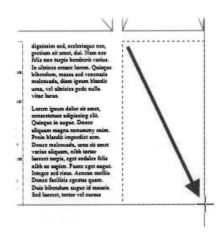

5. The linked frame is created when you release the mouse button, and is filled with the overflowing story text from the previous frames.

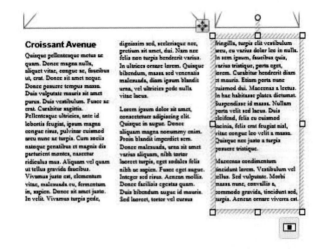

Notice that the frame now displays a 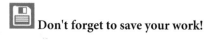 **No Overflow** button, indicating that all of the story text is now displayed.

If you click in either of the first two frames, a 🖵 **Continued** button displays indicating that the frames are linked and that the complete story text is displayed in one or more linked frames.

🖫 **Don't forget to save your work!**

Working with text frames

In the previous example, we created a three column layout using three linked frames. However, a single frame can have multiple columns. This can help simplify the layout design as it takes the worry out of aligning multiple frames. Let's look at this now.

To change the frame layout:

1. On the **Assets** tab, the **Pages** category should be displayed (if not, click the **Pages** header).

2. Drag the **2** page thumbnail to the right of the current page.

    When an arrow appears pointing to the right, release the mouse button to place the page.

    The new page displays automatically.

3. Click once in the text frame to select it.

4.   On the context toolbar, set the column number to **2**.

The text frame updates to contain two columns.

 Don't forget to save your work!

Getting creative with frames

For our next example, we'll show you how to make your frame a little more creative by adding some colour.

To create a colour-filled text frame:

1. Click to select the picture frame (for alignment purposes), and then, on the **Tools** toolbar, click 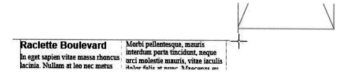 **Standard Text Frame**.

2. Move the cursor in line with the top of the first frame. A set of dynamic guides appear when the cursor is correctly positioned.

Raclette Boulevard
In eget sapien vitae massa rhoncus lacinia. Nullam at leo nec metus

Morbi pellentesque, mauris interdum porta tincidunt, neque orci molestie mauris, vitae iaculis dolor felis at nunc. Maecenas eu

3. Drag across and down the page until a dynamic guide and a page margin guide appear.

The frame is created when you release the mouse button.

4. Select the border of the frame (it will change to a solid outline).

5. On the **Swatches** tab:

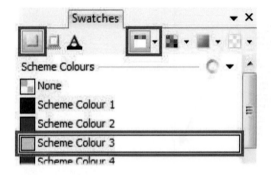

- Click the ▬ **Fill** button.

- From the ▭ **Publication Palette** flyout, select **Scheme Colours**.

- Click the **Scheme Colour 3** swatch.

  The fill is applied.

Now let's add some text...

To insert and format text using text styles:

1. Click inside the text frame to create an insertion point, and then type "Dessert Tour".

2. On the **Text Styles** tab:

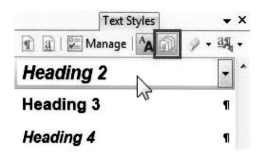

- Click the ▭ **Show All** button.

- Click **Heading 2**.

  The heading style is applied.

If you use styles to format text, you have the advantage that if you want to change the style, all instances of that formatting also update.

Notice that the text is tight against the frame edge? Although this is what we want normally in a frame, as this is a coloured frame, it would look better if we added some internal padding to the frame edge.

To add frame padding:

1. With the text frame still selected, on the context toolbar, click **Text frame setup**.

2.   In the **Frame Setup** dialog:

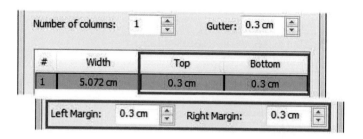

*   Set the **Top** and **Bottom** to **0.3 cm**.

*   Set the **Left Margin** to **0.3 cm**.

*   Set the **Right Margin** to **0.3 cm**.

*   Click **OK**.

     The frame is updated.

Our text frame looks rather bare and would look much better if it displayed some content. PagePlus comes with a handy shortcut to populate text frames with text, so you can quickly visualize text on the page! Let's try this now.

To create placeholder text:

1.   Click inside the text frame at the end of the word "Tour" and press the **Enter** key to drop to the next line.

2.   On the **Insert** menu, click **Fill with Placeholder Text** (or press **F5**).

The text frame is instantly filled with text which approximates the layout of publication text.

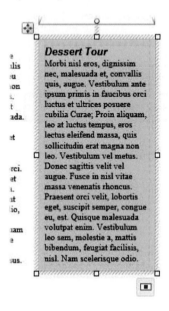

That's it! You now know how to edit and format text, create new frame text objects, and edit text frame properties.

For more detailed information, search *Fitting text to frames* in PagePlus Help.

 Don't forget to save your work!

Assets

 25-30 min

The **Assets** tab in PagePlus X7 hosts a wide variety of designs and objects to help you easily and quickly enhance your publications.

By the end of this tutorial you will be able to:

- Place and use picture frame assets.

- Place graphic assets.

- Add page content assets.

- Add a page asset.

- Adding inline objects.

> If you have already completed the *Frame text* tutorial on p. 27, you can use your saved publication for this tutorial.

> Some of the assets used in this tutorial are only available from the full (default) install of PagePlus.

Let's begin...

1. On the **File** menu, click **Startup Assistant**.

2. On the left, click **New Publication**.

3. Click to select **A4** or **Letter** size paper.

    A single, blank page will open in the workspace.

 Save now! Click **File** > **Save As** and type a new file name.

Using Picture Frame assets

PagePlus comes with a variety of installed Asset Packs. These contain assets (objects or page elements) that can be used to quickly and efficiently build or enhance any publication.

We'll start by looking at picture frames assets. *Pictures* (on p. 13) discusses how to use blank frames, however, the Asset Packs contain frames with creative borders that can really enhance your publication.

Before you can use an asset in your publication, you need to import it into the **Assets** tab.

To add Picture Frame assets to the Assets tab:

1. On the **Assets** tab, click 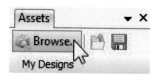 **Browse** to open the **Asset Browser**.

2. In the **Categories** section, click to select the **Picture Frames** category. The picture frames from all installed packs are displayed in the main pane.

3. In the main pane, the assets are categorized by the Pack file that they belong to. In the **Essentials** pack, click the ⊘ **Add All** button. The assets are imported into the **Assets** tab.

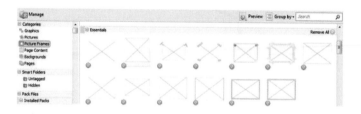

The green ⊘ shows that the asset has been added to the tab.

4. Click **Close** to exit.

To add a picture frame to the page:

1. On the **Assets** tab, the **Picture Frames** category should be displayed (if not, click the **Picture Frames** header).

2. Scroll through the frames, select the one with push pins and then drag it onto the page.

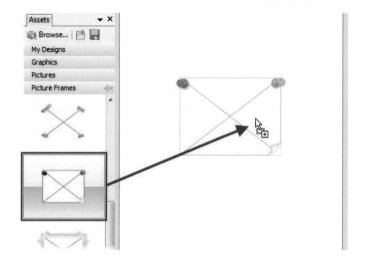

The frame is added to the page at its default size.

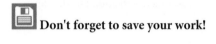 **Don't forget to save your work!**

We'll now add one of the installed Picture assets to the frame.

To add a picture asset to the Assets tab:

1. On the **Assets** tab, click 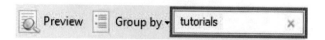 **Browse** to open the **Asset Browser**.

2. In the **Categories** section, click to select the **Pictures** category. The pictures from all installed packs are displayed in the main pane.

3. In the Search box, type "tutorials".

All pictures with the "Tutorials" tag are displayed.

4. Click to select a picture of your choice and then click **Close** to exit.

To add a picture to an existing frame:

1. On the **Assets** tab, the **Pictures** category should be displayed (if not, click the **Pictures** header).

2. Drag the picture onto the picture frame.

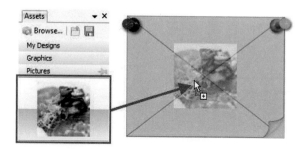

The picture is cropped to fit the frame boundary.

When a picture is placed inside a frame, it's easy to change the frame just by dropping a new one on top of the existing frame.

To swap a picture frame:

1. On the **Assets** tab, click the **Picture Frames** category header.

2. Drag the penultimate picture frame thumbnail from the tab and drop it onto the picture.

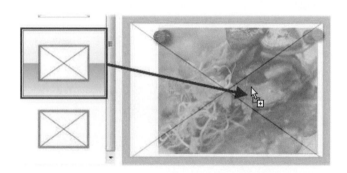

The frame is updated.

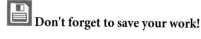 To edit the position of the image inside the frame, use the tools on the picture frame toolbar located beneath the frame when the frame is selected. For more information, see *Pictures* on p. 13.

Don't forget to save your work!

Using graphic assets

Graphic assets can be used to add interest to a page. They are added to the **Assets** tab in exactly the same way as picture frame assets.

To add graphic assets to the Assets tab:

1.   On the **Assets** tab, click **Browse** to open the **Asset Browser**.

2. In the **Categories** section, click to select the **Graphics** category. The graphics from all installed packs are displayed in the main pane.

3. In the Search box, type "ribbon". All graphics with the "ribbon" tag are displayed. Click to select the third **Good Morning** graphic.

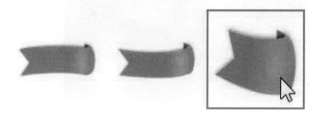

The green  shows that the asset has been added to the tab.

4. In the Search box, click the cross to clear the tag.

5. Type "stag" and click on the displayed graphic.

6. In the Search box, click the cross to clear the tag.

7. Type "globose star" and click on the central graphic.

8. Click **Close** to exit.

To add a graphic to the page:

1. On the **Assets** tab, the **Graphics** category should be displayed
    (if not, click the **Graphics** header).

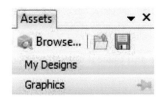

2.   Drag the ribbon graphic to the page (as you did with the picture frame asset) and position it to look like it is wrapping around the picture frame.

Some graphics, such as the ribbon and star graphics, are automatically schemed and will adopt the appropriate colour, while other graphics, such as the stag graphic, are independently coloured.

3.   Drag the stag graphic to the page and place it over the top left corner of the picture frame.

4. With the graphic still selected, on the **Colours** toolbar, from the Fill flyout, select **Scheme Colour 2**.

The graphic immediately adopts the scheme colour.

The **Colours** toolbar will remember the last **Fill**, **Line** and **Text** colour selected so you can quickly apply identical colours later in your project.

5. (Optional) Add and rotate another ribbon graphic, placing it to wrap around the picture frame.

Specialist   **Logo** graphics behave differently to ordinary graphics and have unique properties. Logo assets are covered in detail in *Logos* on p. 67.

Using Page Content assets

Page Content assets are pre-assembled using various page objects, such as artistic text, text frames and blank picture frames. They can be added to your publications to quickly build up the content on pages.

We'll add a pre-assembled contact details asset to the final page of our publication.

To add page content assets to the Assets tab:

1. On the **Assets** tab, click **Browse** to open the **Asset Browser**.

2. In the **Categories** section, click to select the **Page Content** category. The page content from all installed packs are displayed in the main pane.

3. In the Search box, type "User Details". All page content with the "User Details" tag are displayed.

4. Click to select the **Pop** page content.

    The green shows that the asset has been added to the tab.

5. Click **Close** to exit.

To add page content to the page:

1. On the **Assets** tab, the **Page Content** category should be displayed (if not, click the **Page Content** header).

2. Drag the User Details page content to the page.

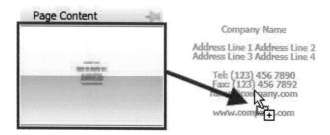

The company details stored in the **User Details** are inserted on the page.

Once the page content has been placed on the page, you can edit and customize it to meet your needs. We centred the text frame horizontally on the page using the **Align** tab.

 To update User Details, from the Tools menu, select Set User Details. Search *Inserting user details* in PagePlus Help for more information.

Next, we'll move onto the Page asset category, as well as looking at adding a graphic in line with text.

 Don't forget to save your work!

Adding a Page asset

For this section, we'll use an asset found in the **Tutorials** assets pack.

To add tutorial assets to the Assets tab:

1. On the **Assets** tab, click ![icon] **Browse** to open the **Asset Browser**.

2. In the **Pack Files** section, select the **Tutorials** pack.

3. In the main pane, the assets are categorized by the category they belong to. In the **Pages** category, click page **1A**.

 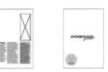

The green ⊘ shows that the asset has been added to the tab.

4. Click **Close** to exit.

Now we'll add the Page asset to our publication.

To add a new Page asset:

1. On the **Assets** tab, the **Pages** category should be displayed (if not, click the **Pages** header).

2. Drag the **1A** page thumbnail to the right of the current page.

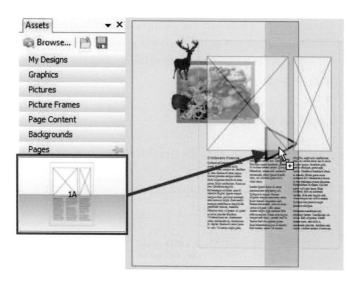

When an arrow appears pointing to the right, release the mouse button to place the page.

The new page displays automatically.

 If you drag the Page asset **onto** the page, it will replace everything on the current page.

 Don't forget to save your work!

Adding an object in line

If you are working with text and pictures in a publication, you can obtain fine control over object positioning using object anchoring. We'll introduce this by adding a small inline image to a section of text on the page.

To add an inline image:

1. On the **Assets** tab, click the **Graphics** category header.

2. Drag the 'globose star' graphic onto the page, placing the cursor within the third text frame.

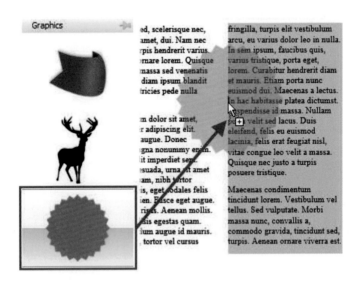

Notice that the frame glows to show that the graphic will be placed inside it.

3.   On release, you will receive a message notifying you that the
     graphic is too large for the frame. You can either:

  •   Click **Yes** to automatically shrink the graphic to fit the text
      frame. The text automatically wraps around it.

  •   Click **No** to abort the addition of the graphic.

  •   Click **Cancel** to place it as a detached graphic.

You can update any object's properties from being **detached** to **floating** or
vice versa. To do so, select the object and, from the **Arrange** menu, click
Anchor Object. Search *Adding anchors to objects* in PagePlus Help for more
details.

Whichever placement option you chose, you can adjust the object's wrap settings to suit your needs—we've supplied two suggestions depending on whether the object is floating (see below) or detached (p. 64).

To adjust wrap settings of a floating object:

1. Click the graphic to select it.

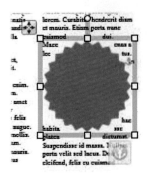

2. On the **Arrange** toolbar, click **Wrap Settings**.

3. In the **Wrap Settings** dialog:

    •   In the **Wrapping** section, select **Square**.

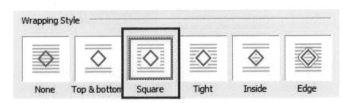

- In the **Distance from text** section, enter **0.3 cm** in all four of the value boxes.

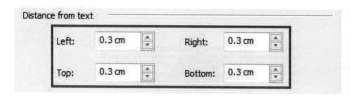

- Click **OK**.

Alternatively, for a detached object...

To adjust wrap settings of a detached object:

1. Click the graphic to select it.

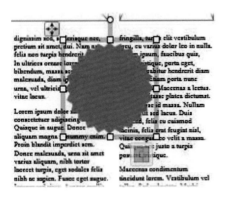

2. On the **Arrange** toolbar, click ⬜ **Wrap Settings**.

3. In the **Wrap Settings** dialog:

    • In the **Wrapping** section, select **Tight**.

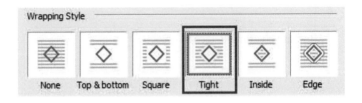

    • In the **Distance from text** section, enter **0.3 cm** in all four
       of the value boxes

- Click **OK**.

 Don't forget to save your work!

That's it! You've successfully added a range of assets to your publication.

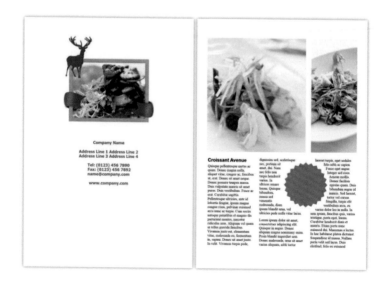

Custom graphics, pictures, picture frames, page content, backgrounds and publication pages can all be stored in the Assets tab for later use. Search *Storing designs* in PagePlus Help for more information.

There's so much more you can do!

Below is an example of what else you can do...

Add a background asset

Background assets quickly transform your publications. They are added to the Assets tab and applied to your page in the same way as the assets discussed in this tutorial. See *Master pages* on p. 77 for more information.

Logos

15-20 min

Logos provide a great way of quickly identifying your business, club or charity. The Logo assets provided with PagePlus help you easily establish your brand with no design skills necessary. Alternatively, you can use the LogoStudio to create or edit your company logo.

By the end of this tutorial you will be able to:

- Use the installed logo assets.

- Modify an existing logo.

- Create your own logo.

- Add a logo design to the Assets tab.

Let's begin...

1. On the **File** menu, click **Startup Assistant**.

2. On the left, click **New Publication**.

3. Click to select **A4** or **Letter** size paper.

    A single, blank page will open in the workspace.

Using the Logo assets

Next, we'll have a look at adding our first logo to the page.

To import logos to the Assets tab:

1. On the **Assets** tab, click the **Graphics** category header and then
    click 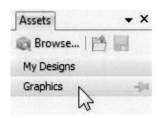 **Browse**.

2. In the **Asset Browser** dialog, in the search box, type "logo".

    All of the pre-designed logos are displayed.

3. Click on the thumbnail of each of the logos that you want to import to the **Assets** tab.

    (To import all of the logos, click ⊘ **Add All**.)

4. When you've selected the logos you want, click **Close**.

    Your selected logos will be marked 🖢 and displayed in the **Graphics** category of the **Assets** tab, ready for adding to your publication.

To insert a logo on the page:

1. Drag a logo from the **Graphics** category of the **Assets** tab to the page.

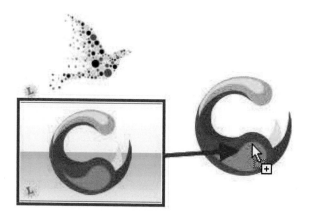

2. In the **Insert Logo** dialog:

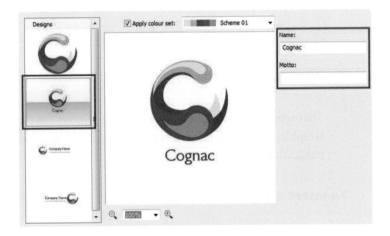

- In the **Designs** pane, choose your design.

- In the **Name** text box, type your company name.

- Amend the **Motto** text—we removed all the motto text.

- To apply a colour set (a specially designed logo scheme), select the **Apply colour set** check box, and then select a colour set from the drop-down list.

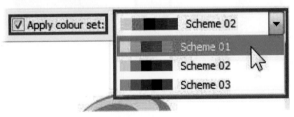

- or -

- To apply the colour scheme of the publication, clear the **Apply colour set** check box.

- Click **OK**.

3. The logo is placed on the page and you can now move it into place and resize as necessary.

 **Save now!** Click **File** > **Save As** and type a new file name.

Editing an existing logo asset

One of the best things about the logos in PagePlus is that they can be customized to get that tailored look for your publications. This can be done in LogoStudio. Let's have a look at this now.

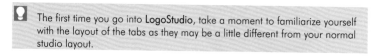 The first time you go into **LogoStudio**, take a moment to familiarize yourself with the layout of the tabs as they may be a little different from your normal studio layout.

To edit an existing logo:

1. Click the ☑ **Edit in LogoStudio** button that displays on the control bar under the selected logo.

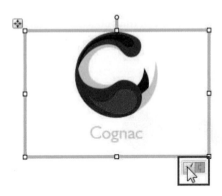

2. LogoStudio opens with your object(s) zoomed in to fit your workspace.

3. To customize your logo design, use the interactive **How To** tab elements, or the traditional PagePlus creation tools.

4. Click ✕ **Close LogoStudio** to return to the main PagePlus workspace and view your logo on the page.

In this logo we changed the text's format and repositioned it. We also deleted some of the shapes and reassigned some scheme colours.

Creating your own logos

PagePlus also makes it very easy to create your own logos.

To convert an existing design to a logo:

1. Select the object(s) you want to convert to your logo.

2. On the **Tools** menu, click **Convert To > Logo**.

Your design is converted to a logo and can now be edited in LogoStudio.

 Don't forget to save your work!

To create a logo from scratch in the LogoStudio:

1. On the **Insert** menu, click **Logo**.

2. Click (or drag) to place the logo on the page.

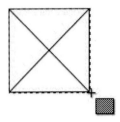

The LogoStudio environment opens automatically.

3. To create your design, you can use the interactive **How To** tab elements, or the traditional PagePlus creation tools.

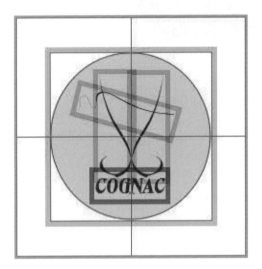

To make it easier to align our objects, we clicked ▊▊ Clean Design to temporarily disable clean design mode and turn on the layout guides. This button toggles the display so if the guides are already displayed, clicking the button again will hide them.

4. To return to your original publication, click ⊗ **Close LogoStudio**. Your design is displayed on page.

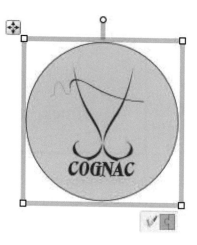

💾 **Don't forget to save your work!**

Adding your design to the Assets tab

When you've completed your logo design, why not add it to the **Assets** tab so that it's readily accessible for use in all of your publications?

To add a logo to the Assets tab:

1. On the **Assets** tab, click the **My Designs** category header.

2. Simply drag your design into the **Assets** tab.

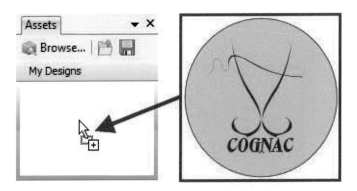

A copy of the design is displayed in the **My Designs** section of the **Assets** tab and is now ready for use in all of your future projects!

We hope that you've enjoyed this adventure into logo territory and feel confident in using them throughout your publications. Have fun!

Master pages

 20-25 min

Some elements of your design will appear on every page of your publication. By using master pages, publication pages can share the same underlying design. This allows you to achieve consistency throughout your publication, and save yourself a lot of time and effort in the process!

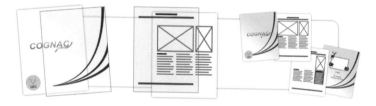

By the end of this tutorial you will be able to:

* Create and use a master page.

* Draw straight lines on a page.

* Create a second master page.

* Assign alternative master pages to a page.

> If you have already completed the *Pictures* (p. 13), *Frame text* (p. 27), or *Assets* (p. 45) tutorials, you can use your saved publication for this tutorial.

Let's begin...

1.   On the **File** menu, click **Startup Assistant**.

2.   On the left, click **New Publication**.

3.   Click to select **A4** or **Letter** size paper.

     A single, blank page will open in the workspace.

Before we delve into using master pages, let's build a quick publication using Pages assets.

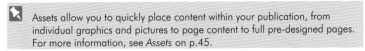

Assets allow you to quickly place content within your publication, from individual graphics and pictures to page content to full pre-designed pages. For more information, see *Assets* on p.45.

For this tutorial, we'll use some of the assets found in the **Tutorials** assets pack.

To add tutorial assets to the Assets tab:

1.   On the **Assets** tab, click Browse to open the **Asset Browser**.

2.   In the **Pack Files** section, select the **Tutorials** pack.

3.   In the main pane, the assets are categorized by the category they belong to. In the **Pages** category, click pages **1A** , **2A**, **3** and **4**. (Page names appear as tooltips.)

4.   Click **Close** to exit.

To add a Pages asset to the publication:

1.   On the **Assets** tab, the **Pages** category should be displayed (if not, click the **Pages** header).

2.   Drag the **3** page thumbnail onto the page.

3.   Drag the **1A** page thumbnail to the right of the current page.

When an arrow appears pointing to the right, release the mouse button to place the page.

The new page displays automatically.

> ⚠ If you drag the Page asset **onto** the page, it will replace everything on the current page.

4.   Repeat step 3 to add **2A** and **4** page assets to your publication.

The pages are now visible in the **Pages** tab.

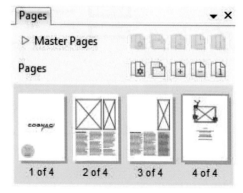

Save now! Click **File** > **Save As** and type a new file name.

Why use master pages?

Master pages are like sheets of transparent paper located behind or in front of your main publication pages. Every page can have one or more master pages assigned to it and a given master page can be shared by any number of main pages.

Creating a consistent design is simple when you use a master page. When you add text frames, pictures, or other elements to the master page, they appear in the same position on all publication pages that use that master page. This makes it easy to create a consistent design throughout your publication.

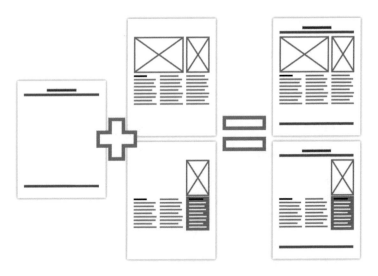

What you place on a master page is entirely up to you and often depends on the type of publication you are creating. Typical elements that you'd place on a master page include:

- background pictures (patterns, watermarks, etc.).

- company name and/or logo.

- page number (using an automatic field—for more details, see *Page numbering* on p. 155).

- contact details.

Master pages simplify publication maintenance as objects placed on a master page only need updating once. (If you didn't use a master page, you'd have to update the object on each individual page of the publication.)

Creating a master page (Master A)

Before we start, take a moment to familiarize yourself with the publication layout by double-clicking the pages in the **Pages** tab.

As you can see, each page has content but it is all placed on a plain background. By using a master page, we can edit all of the pages at once! Let's look at this first.

To access master pages:

1.   On the **Pages** tab, click **Master Pages** to show the Master Pages pane. The publication currently has a single, blank master page.

2. Double-click **MasterA** page thumbnail to display the page in the workspace.

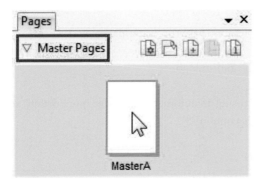

The page in the workspace resembles an ordinary page. However, any objects which are placed on this page will automatically appear on every page in your publication. Let's try this out by adding a couple of basic straight lines.

To add lines to a page:

1. On the **Tools** toolbar, select the **Straight Line Tool**.

2. Position your cursor on the left side of the page where the blue margin guide appears.

3. Drag horizontally across the page until the blue margin guide on the right side appears.

> To get a perfectly horizontal line by constraining the line's angle, hold down the Shift key as you drag.

4. On the **Colours** toolbar, from the 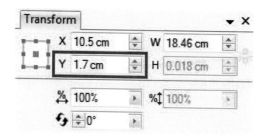 **Line** flyout, select **Scheme Colour 1**.

> The Colours toolbar will remember the last Fill, Line and Text colour selected so you can quickly apply identical colours later in your project.

5. On the **Transform** tab, set the **Y** position to **1.7 cm**.

Transform		▼ ✕
X 10.5 cm	W 18.46 cm	
Y 1.7 cm	H 0.018 cm	
100%	%‡ 100%	
⟳ 0°		

6. Repeat steps 2-4 to add a second straight line to your page, and then, on the **Transform** tab, set the **Y** position to **28.0 cm**.

You now have two neat lines on your master page.

Next we'll add some artistic text to our master page design.

. For more information on adding and modifying artistic text, see *Artistic text on p. 3.*

 Save now! Click **File > Save As** and type a new file name.

To add artistic text:

1. On the **Tools** toolbar, click the $\mathbf{A}$ **Artistic Text Tool**.

2. Click above the top straight line when the blue margin line appears.

3. On the context toolbar, from the styles drop-down list, select **Heading 1**.

4. On the **Insert** menu, select **Information > User Details**.

5. In the **User Details** dialog, select **(Business) Company** and click **OK**.

6. Click the border of the artistic text object (it will turn solid), then on the **Colours** toolbar, from the $\mathbf{\underline{A}}$ **Text** flyout, select **Scheme Colour 2**.

7. On the **Align** tab:

- From the **Relative to** drop-down list, select **Page**.

- Click 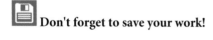 **Centre Horizontally**.

Your master page should now resemble ours...

We updated our User Details for a company called 'Cognac'—the company name automatically updates. To update **User Details**, from the **Tools** menu, select **Set User Details**. Search *Inserting user details* in PagePlus Help for more information.

Don't forget to save your work!

Let's apply this master page to all our publication pages and then see how it looks!

To apply a master page to all pages:

1. On the **Pages** tab, on the Master Pages pane, right-click **MasterA** page thumbnail and select **Apply to** > **All pages**.

2. On the **Pages** tab, on the Pages pane, double-click a standard, publication page thumbnail.

3. Click through pages on the **Pages** tab, or click the arrows on the **Hintline** toolbar, to view the pages.

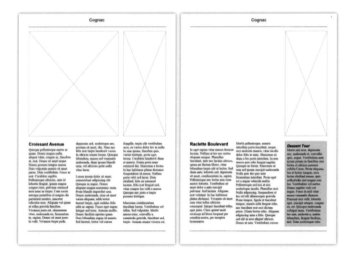

As you can see, the lines and artistic text placed on the master page display on all the standard pages.

Additional master pages

The design suits the inner pages well, but it does not suit the front or
back pages very well. What we need is a different design for the front
and back pages. We can easily do this by creating a second master
page!

To create a second master page:

1. On the **Pages** tab, on the Master Pages pane, double-click the
    'MasterA' page thumbnail to display the page in the workspace.

2. Click ⬚ **Master Page Manager** and in the **Master Page
    Manager** dialog:

    *   Select the **Add** tab.

    *   Click **OK**.

A new master page, **MasterB**, is displayed in the workspace and as a
thumbnail in the **Pages** tab.

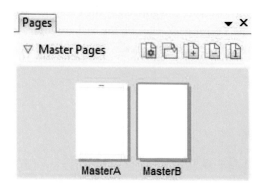

> If you have landscape and portrait pages in your publication, you can change the orientation of a master page to match.
>
> • On the **Pages** tab, on the Master Pages pane, select the appropriate master page thumbnail.
> • Click 🖹 **Change Page Orientation**. The master page updates.

We'll use a background asset to quickly design our new master page. First we need to add the background asset to the Assets tab.

To add Background assets to the Assets tab:

1. On the **Assets** tab, click 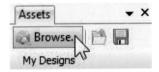 **Browse** to open the **Asset Browser**.

2. In the **Categories** section, click to select the **Backgrounds** category. The backgrounds from all installed packs are displayed in the main pane.

3. In the main pane, the assets are categorized by the Pack file that they belong to. In the **Vector** pack, click on the background thumbnail containing three vanishing arcs.

4. Click **Close** to exit.

Now that we have imported our background, we can add it to the page.

To add a background to the page:

1. On the **Assets** tab, the **Backgrounds** category should be displayed (if not, click the **Backgrounds** header).

2. Drag the background onto the page.

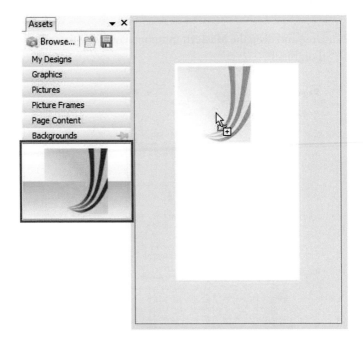

The background is added to the page as a special background layer and automatically adjusts to fit the page area.

You can change to a different background at any time by simply dragging a different background from the **Assets** tab onto the page.

Now we've completed our second master page design, we need to assign it to the front and back pages of our publication.

 Don't forget to save your work!

To assign a master page:

1. On the **Pages** tab, double-click on the first page thumbnail (1 of 4) to return to normal view.

2. Drag and drop the **MasterB** thumbnail onto the first page thumbnail.

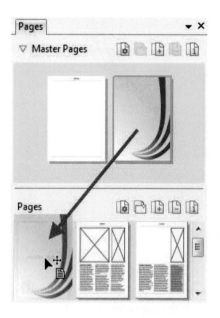

The master page is assigned.

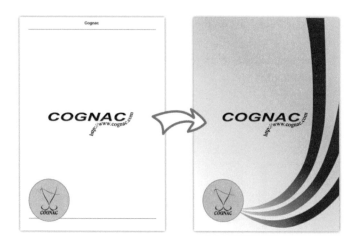

3. Repeat step 2 to assign **Master B** to the last page.

To check master page assignment:

1. On the **Pages** tab, on the Pages pane, click 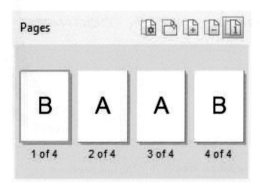 **Page Identifiers**.

    The assigned master pages are displayed on each page thumbnail.

2. Click the button again to return to the normal thumbnail view.

That's it! You have successfully created and assigned multiple master pages to a publication.

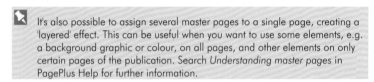

It's also possible to assign several master pages to a single page, creating a 'layered' effect. This can be useful when you want to use some elements, e.g. a background graphic or colour, on all pages, and other elements on only certain pages of the publication. Search *Understanding master pages* in PagePlus Help for further information.

Tables

15-20 min

Tables are a great way of displaying all forms of data quickly and easily. Price lists, opening times, menus, school timetables, and financial and research data in particular—all look best when inserted into a table in your publication. The best part is that PagePlus makes this easy to do.

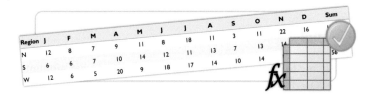

By the end of this tutorial you will be able to:

- Create a table.

- Populate a table with data.

- Add and delete rows and columns.

- Add a standard SUM function.

- Format the appearance of your table.

Let's begin...

1. On the **File** menu, click **Startup Assistant**.

2. On the left, click **New Publication**.

3. From the **Landscape** category, click to select **A4** or **Letter** size paper.

   A single, blank page will open in the workspace.

Creating a table

We're going to create a table which is ideal for displaying 'amounts' of data. The data could represent a range of things from new membership numbers to product sales, depending on your specific needs, tracked over a twelve month period. To make it more dynamic, we'll also track the data from three different regions.

To create a table:

1. On the **Tools** toolbar, click the **Table Tool**.

2. Position your mouse pointer near the top left of the page where the margin guides appear.

3.　Drag to create a table which stretches to the right margin guide and is **4cm** high.

The Hintline toolbar displays the size as you drag.

Table: Shift-drag to constrain to a square. Pos: (1.27 cm, 1.27 cm) | Size: (27.16 cm, 3.962 cm)

4.　In the **Create Table** dialog:

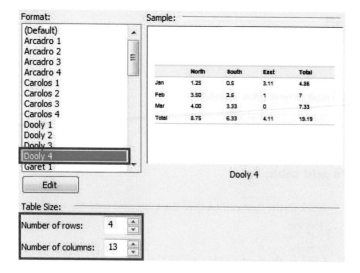

- In the **Format** list, click **Dooly 4**.

- Set the **Number of rows** to **4**.

- Set the **Number of columns** to **13**.

- Click **OK**.

The table is added to the page and formatted as selected above.

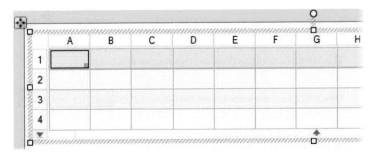

Save now! Click **File > Save As** and type a new file name.

Populating the table

Let's now add our information to the table.

To add table data:

1. Click in the first cell (**A1**) of the table and type the word 'Region'.

2. Click in the next header cell (**B1**) and type 'J' (for January) and then press the right arrow key. Notice that the cursor moves to the next available cell (i.e. **C1**).

3. Repeat the above step to add the months February through to December.

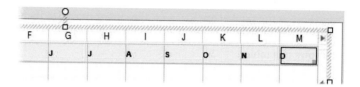

4. Press the right arrow key.

   Notice that the cursor moves to the next available cell—in this case, **A2**.

5. Type 'N' (for North) and then press the down arrow key.

   Notice that the cursor moves to the cell below (i.e. **A3**).

6. Repeat the above step to add 'S' and 'W' (for South and West, respectively).

7. Fill the table with any numerical data you have available.

With the data now added, let's have a look at how you can modify the table.

Region	J	F	M	A	M	J	J	A	S	O	N	D
N	12	8	7	9	11	8	18	11	3	11	22	16
S	6	6	7	10	14	12	11	13	7	13	14	10
W	12	6	5	20	9	18	17	14	10	14	13	18

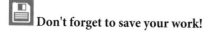 **Don't forget to save your work!**

Modifying the table

When working inside tables, the **Tab** key exhibits the same behaviour as the right arrow key—i.e. the cursor moves to the next available cell. However, unlike the right arrow key, it can also create new rows in a table.

 Pressing **Shift-Tab** exhibits the same behaviour as the left arrow key, i.e. it moves the cursor to the previous available cell, but does not exhibit the Tab key behaviour described below.

To add a table row:

- Click in the last (bottom right) cell of the table and then press the **Tab** key.

  A new row is added to the table and the cursor moves to the first cell in this new row.

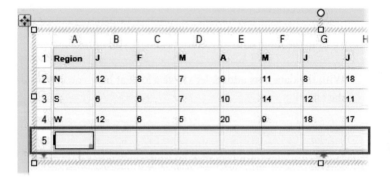

You can add an additional **Region** label (such as 'E' for East) and further data if required, but as we don't currently need this row, we'll show you how to delete it.

To delete table row(s):

1. Click inside the first cell that you want to delete and then drag over the other twelve empty cells.

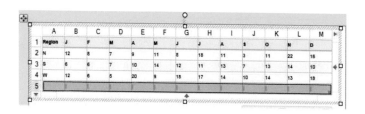

2. On the **Table** menu, click **Delete > Row(s)**.

    The rows are deleted from the table.

We'll now show you how to add a column to your table.

To add a column:

1. With your table selected, click on the column header **M**. The whole column is highlighted.

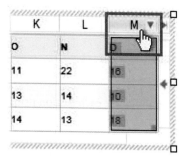

2. On the **Table** menu, click **Insert > Columns**.

3. In the **Insert Columns** dialog, select the **After selected cells** option and click **OK**.

   A new column is added to the right of the table.

   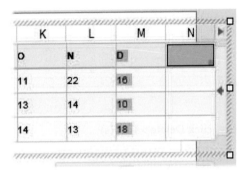

   You'll notice the table now extends beyond the page area onto the pasteboard. We'll correct this.

4. Drag the right middle selection handle inwards until the edge of the table lines up with the margin guide.

   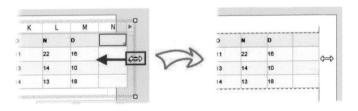

We'll use this new column to create a total for each Region using a formula.

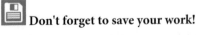 **Don't forget to save your work!**

Using formulas

As well as storing standard text and numerical content, PagePlus tables also have the ability to hold calculating formulas and functions. We'll look at the standard SUM function.

To add a table function:

1. Click inside the first cell of column **N** and type 'Sum' and then press the down arrow key.

2. On the context toolbar, click *fx* **Spreadsheet Functions**.

    The Table toolbar displays.

3. On the **Table** toolbar:

    •   From the *fx* ▾ **Function flyout**, select **SUM()**.

        The spreadsheet function box will automatically update with the appropriate formula.

        The formula tells PagePlus to add up all the values within the brackets (parenthesis)—in the above case, the values from B2 to M2.

- Click  **Accept** to place the formula in the selected cell.

| 11 | 8 | 18 | 11 | 3 | 11 | 22 | 16 | =sum(B 2:M2) |

Cells B2-M2 are highlighted to show they are used in a calculation.

4. Click inside cell **N3** and on the **Table** toolbar:

   - In the spreadsheet function box, type '=sum(' and then drag to select cells B3-M3.

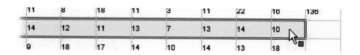

   - Click  **Accept** to place the formula in the selected cell.

5. Click inside cell **N4** and on the **Table** toolbar:

   - In the spreadsheet function box, type '=sum(B4:M4)'.

   - Click  **Accept** to place the formula in the selected cell.

PagePlus calculates the totals from your data and presents them in the final column of the table.

Region	J	F	M	A	M	J	J	A	S	O	N	D	Sum
N	12	8	7	9	11	8	18	11	3	11	22	16	136
S	6	6	7	10	14	12	11	13	7	13	14	10	123
W	12	6	5	20	9	18	17	14	10	14	13	18	156

Formatting the table

You don't have to stick with the table formatting you originally chose for your table. You can apply another preset design at any point during design.

To apply a table Auto Format:

1. Click on the table to select it.

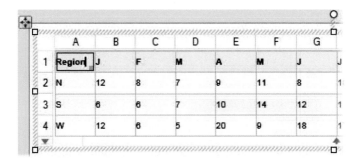

2. On the context toolbar, click 🖾 **Auto Format**.

3. In the **AutoFormat** dialog:

    • In the **Format** list, click **Garet 4**.

    • Click **OK**.

The new AutoFormat table format is applied.

Region	J	F	M	A	M	J	J	A	S	O	N	D	Sum
N	12	8	7	9	11	8	18	11	3	11	22	16	136
S	6	6	7	10	14	12	11	13	7	13	14	10	123
W	12	6	5	20	9	18	17	14	10	14	13	18	156

You can also customize the AutoFormat table format and save it for use in other publications.

To create a custom table format:

1. With the table selected, on the **Table** menu, click **Edit AutoFormat**.

   The **Table Formats** dialog opens, ready to edit the currently applied table format.

2. In the **Cell Style** list, click **Header** and then click **Edit**.

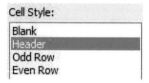

3. In the **Cell Properties** dialog:

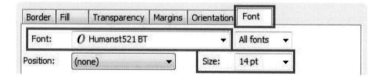

   • Click the **Font** tab.

   • From the **Font** drop-down list, select **Humans521 BT**.

   • From the **Size** drop-down list, select **14 pt**.

* Click **OK**.

  The changes are displayed in the Preview pane.

4. Repeat steps 2 and 3 to edit the **Odd Row** and **Even Row** styles.

5. Click **Save As**.

6. Type a name for your new format and click **OK**.

7. Finally, click **OK** to close the **Table Formats** dialog.

Your table is updated with the new format.

Region	J	F	M	A	M	J	J	A	S	O	N	D	Sum
N	12	8	7	9	11	8	18	11	3	11	22	16	136
S	6	6	7	10	14	12	11	13	7	13	14	10	123
W	12	6	5	20	9	18	17	14	10	14	13	18	156

 By formatting the table in this way, you will be able to quickly apply this style to any table in future publications with the **Auto Format** button on the context toolbar.

That's it! You have now created a simple data table which also calculates totals.

Don't forget to save your work!

There's so much more you can do!

Create charts

You can use the data in your table to create a variety of stunning charts—perfect for presentations and corporate brochures. See *Charts* on the following page for more information.

Create a calendar

Why not create your own calendar with the  **Calendar Tool**? A Wizard will guide you through the initial setup and the formatting techniques are very similar to tables. Search *Inserting a calendar* in PagePlus Help for more information.

Charts

 45 min

Charts are visually appealing and, if used correctly, can display data in an extremely precise *and* concise way. Charts are perfect for presentations and corporate brochures and can be used to explain table data effectively.

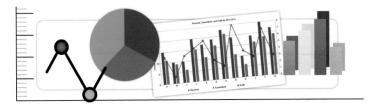

By the end of this tutorial you will be able to:

- Create column, bar, pie, line and hybrid charts.

- Modify chart labels.

- Modify a chart's data range.

- Modify a chart's linked data.

- Modify a chart to display a secondary axis.

If you have already completed the *Tables* tutorial on p. 93, you can use your saved publication for this tutorial.

Let's begin...

1. On the **File** menu, click **Startup Assistant**.

2. On the left, click **New Publication**.

3. From the **Landscape** category, click to select **A4** or **Letter** size paper.

   A single, blank page will open in the workspace.

For this tutorial, we'll use some of the assets found in the **Tutorials** assets pack.

To add tutorial assets to the Assets tab:

1. On the **Assets** tab, click  **Browse** to open the **Asset Browser**.

2. In the **Pack Files** section, select the **Tutorials** pack.

3. In the main pane, the assets are categorized by the category they belong to. In the **Pages** category, click pages **6**, **7** and **8**. (Page names appear as tooltips.)

4. Click **Close** to exit.

To add a Pages asset to the publication:

1. On the **Assets** tab, the **Pages** category should be displayed (if not, click the **Pages** header).

2. Drag the **6** page thumbnail onto the page.

 Save now! Click **File** > **Save As** and type a new file name.

Creating a column chart

We're going to create a chart based on the table displayed at the bottom of the page. The data could represent a range of things from new membership numbers to product sales, depending on your specific needs, tracked over a twelve month period.

To create a chart from a table:

1. Click to select the table and then click on the table's border (it will turn solid).

    You'll notice the table displays its own object toolbar.

2. On the table's object toolbar, click **Chart Tool**.

3. Position your mouse pointer near the top left of the page where the margin guides appear.

4. Drag to create a chart which stretches to the right margin guide. Set the height to approximately **16cm**.

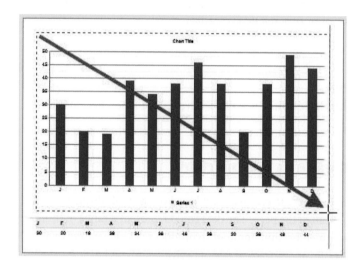

The Hintline toolbar displays the size as you drag.

Chart: Shift-drag to constrain to a square. Pos: (1.27 cm, 1.27 cm) Size: (27.16 cm, 16.012 cm)

The chart is added to the page using the default chart style (Column chart) and placeholder labels.

Let's modify the chart labels to represent a business listing its product sales over a twelve month period.

To modify chart labels:

1. With the chart selected, select the **Charts** tab and click Chart.

2. On the **Chart** pane:

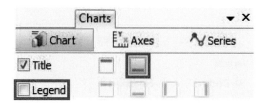

- Deselect the **Legend** option—because there is only one series in this chart, the legend is superfluous.

- Select the option to display the **Title** below the chart.

3. Click to select the Chart Title label on the page and press **Ctrl+A** to select all the default text.

4. Type 'Product Sales: 2013'.

Product Sales: 2013

5. With the chart selected, on the **Charts** tab, click $\overset{EY}{\underset{x}{\boxed{}}}$ **Axes**.

6. On the **Axes** pane, from the **Primary Vertical** options, select **Title**.

An Axis Title label displays on the chart with default text.

7. Click to select the Axis Title label on the page and press **Ctrl+A** to select all the default text.

8. Type 'Product Units Sold'.

The column chart (and first page) is now complete!

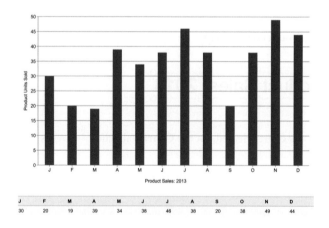

Next we'll take a look at creating a bar chart.

Creating a bar chart

A bar chart will lend itself well to data which has multiple series as you can clearly see comparisons between the different series. We'll use data which could represent product sales tracked over a twelve month period split down into three different regions.

To create a chart linked to a table:

1. On the **Assets** tab, the **Pages** category should be displayed (if not, click the **Pages** header).

2. Drag the **7** page thumbnail to the right of the current page.

    When an arrow appears pointing to the right, release the mouse button to place the page. The new page displays automatically.

> The table on this page was created in the *Tables* tutorial on p. 93.

3. On the **Tools** toolbar, from the Table flyout, select **Chart Tool**.

4. Position your mouse pointer near the top left of the page where the margin guides appear.

5. Drag to create a chart which stretches to the right margin guide. Set the height to approximately **14.4cm**.

    The chart is added to the page using the default chart style (Column chart) and placeholder labels.

6. On the context toolbar:

- From the **Chart** drop-down list, select **Bar**.

- From the **Table** drop-down list, select **Table2**.

The chart updates to display the data from the table below as a bar chart.

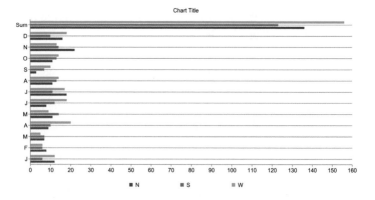

A chart can use data from **any** table in your publication—they don't have to be on the same page! Simply select the table to link to from the context toolbar. Search *Using charts* in PagePlus Help for more information.

Currently the bar chart uses all the data in the table. By including the annual Sum for each region in the chart, the scale is difficult to read. Let's modify the chart to exclude the Sum data and make it more accessible.

To modify linked chart data range:

1. Click once to select the table at the bottom of the page.

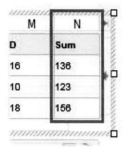

You'll notice the Sum title and values are located in column **N**.

2. Click to select the chart and then, on the **Charts** tab, click Chart.

3. On the **Chart** pane, in the **Range** input box, set the range to **A1:M4**.

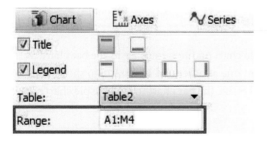

The bar chart updates to display only the specified range.

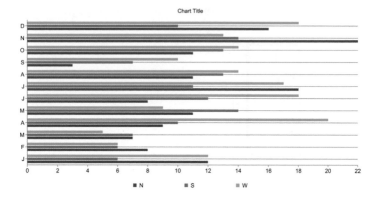

It seems a shame to completely ignore the Sum column in the table. Instead, we can create another chart to better display the information. We'll use a Pie chart.

 Don't forget to save your work!

Creating a pie chart

We'll create the pie chart on the same page as the bar chart, as the charts complement one another and it is useful to show them side-by-side. First we'll resize the bar chart to give the pie chart some space.

To resize a chart:

1. Click to select the bar chart.

2. Drag the right middle selection handle inwards until the chart is approximately **20cm** wide.

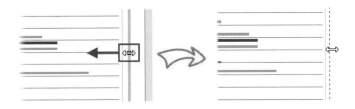

The Hintline toolbar displays the size as you drag.

Now we'll add a second chart to the page.

To create a pie chart:

1. On the **Tools** toolbar, from the Table flyout, select ⅰⅰ **Chart Tool**.

2. Position your mouse pointer to the right of the bar chart where the top margin guides appear.

> With snapping and dynamic guides switched on (default settings), you will see a red dynamic guide appear to help you align the pie chart to the right side of the bar chart.

3. Hold down the **Shift** key and drag to create a chart which stretches to the right margin guide.

The Shift key constrains the chart to a square—perfect for pie charts.

4. On the context toolbar:

- From the **Chart** drop-down list, select **Pie**.

- From the **Table** drop-down list, select **Table2**.

5. On the **Charts** tab, click 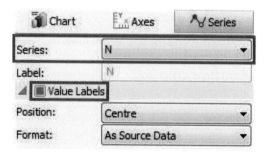 **Series**.

6. On the **Series** pane:

- From the **Series** drop-down list, select **N**.

- Click ☐ to enable the **Value Labels**.

- Repeat the above steps to add value labels to series **S** and **W**.

The chart updates to display the applied settings.

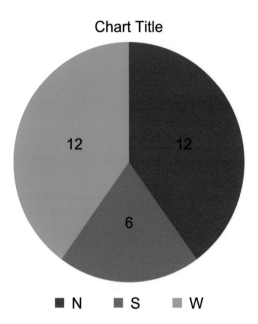

You may have noticed that the pie chart currently displays the data from the **J** (January) column rather than from the **Sum** column. This is because pie charts are only designed to compare a few values and cannot effectively display all the data in the table.

Let's modify the chart's linked data to only include the Sum column from the table.

 Don't forget to save your work!

To modify linked chart data:

1. With the pie chart selected, position your mouse over the **Chart Data** tab flyout.

    The **Chart Data** tab temporarily displays in your workspace.

    > By default, the Chart Data tab is located vertically on the right side of your workspace (see *Exploring PagePlus X7* in the opening pages).

2. On the **Chart Data** tab, from the **Table** drop-down list, select **<none>**.

    This removes the direct link between the chart and the table, but retains the table's data within the Chart Data tab. This allows you to update the data without changing the table on the page.

3. On the **Chart Data** tab, click in any of the cells in the first **J** column and then click **Delete Column**.

4. Repeat step 3 for all the columns until only the **Sum** column remains.

    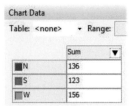

The pie chart updates to display only the data specified in the Chart Data tab.

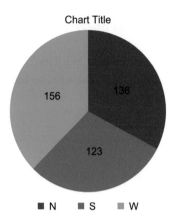

You can update the chart labels and add additional axis labels as detailed in *To modify chart labels* (p. 110) to complete the page. Using the **Align** tab, we also horizontally centred the pie chart with respect to the bar chart.

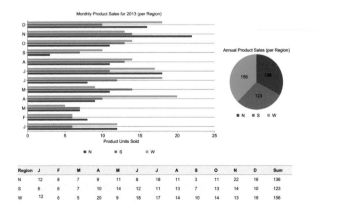

Region	J	F	M	A	M	J	J	A	S	O	N	D	Sum
N	12	8	7	9	11	8	18	11	3	11	22	16	136
S	6	6	7	10	14	12	11	13	7	13	14	10	123
W	12	6	5	20	9	18	17	14	10	14	13	18	156

Next, we'll explore using charts to track data trends.

Creating a line chart to track trends

We'll use a line chart to track some financial data. We'll look specifically at revenue, expenditure, and profit over a twelve month period.

To create a line chart:

1. On the **Assets** tab, the **Pages** category should be displayed (if not, click the **Pages** header).

2. Drag the **8** page thumbnail to the right of the current page.

   When an arrow appears pointing to the right, release the mouse button to place the page.

   The new page displays automatically.

3. Click to select the table and then click on the table's border (it will turn solid).

4. On the table's object toolbar, click **Chart Tool**.

5. Drag to create a chart which stretches to the right margin guide. Set the height to fill the remainder of the page.

   The chart is added to the page using the default chart style (Column chart) and placeholder labels.

6.   With the chart selected, on the **Styles** tab:

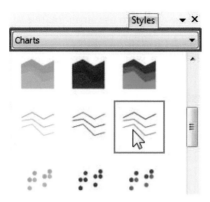

●   From the category drop-down list, select **Charts**.

●   From the **2D** sub-category, click the **Line 03** thumbnail.

The chart adopts the preset line style listed in the Styles tab.

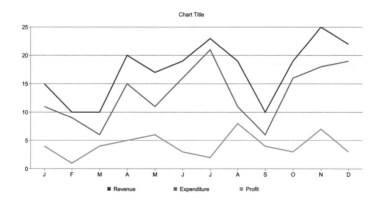

See *Object styles* on p. 141 for more information on working with object styles.

As revenue, expenditure, and profit are all plotted at the same scale it could prove difficult to determine the exact values for the profit in particular. However, we have the option to use an alternative scale for the profit series by creating a secondary vertical axis. Sounds complicated, but PagePlus makes it straightforward.

To add a secondary axis:

1. With the line chart selected, on the **Charts** tab, click 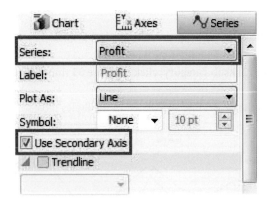 **Series**.

2. On the **Series** pane:

- From the **Series** drop-down list, select **Profit**.

- Select the **Use Secondary Axis** option.

The chart updates to use a 0-25 scale on the left axis and a 0-8 scale on the right axis—with revenue and expenditure plotted on the former and profit on the latter.

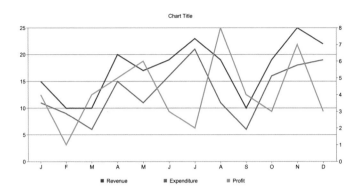

The number of lines and similarity of the colours make it difficult to read this chart. It's also not clear which line is using which vertical axis. We'll correct this by converting the revenue and expenditure lines to columns and changing the profit line colour.

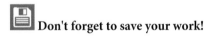 **Don't forget to save your work!**

To create a hybrid chart and change chart colours:

1. With the line chart selected, on the **Charts** tab, click ⋏⋎ **Series**.

2. On the **Series** pane:

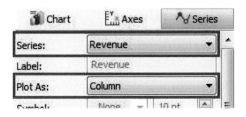

   - From the **Series** drop-down list, select **Revenue**.

- From the **Plot As** drop-down list, select **Column**.

- Repeat the above steps to convert the **Expenditure** series to columns.

- From the **Series** drop-down list, select **Profit**.

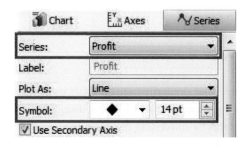

- From the **Symbol** drop-down list, select a symbol marker and set the size to **14pt**.

3. On the **Swatches** tab:

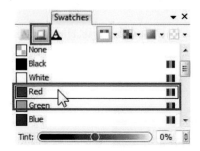

- Ensure **Line** is selected.

- Click a thumbnail to select a contrasting colour from the palette.

The chart updates to display the applied settings.

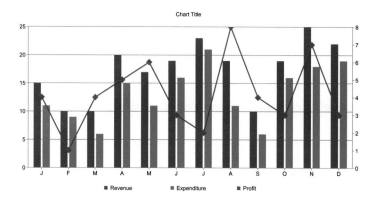

You can update the chart labels and add additional axis labels as detailed in *To modify chart labels* (p. 110) to complete the page.

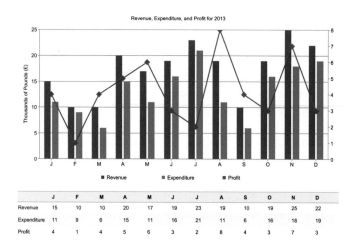

	J	F	M	A	M	J	J	A	S	O	N	D
Revenue	15	10	10	20	17	19	23	19	10	19	25	22
Expenditure	11	9	6	15	11	16	21	11	6	16	18	19
Profit	4	1	4	5	6	3	2	8	4	3	7	3

That's it! You have now created a range of charts and modified them in a variety of ways.

 Don't forget to save your work!

There's so much more you can do!

Below is an example of what else you can do...

Output to PDF slideshow

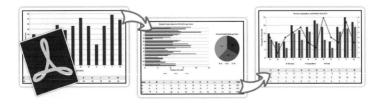

Although your charts will look stunning in a published report or brochure, they are also perfect for use in a presentation. Once your charts have been constructed, you can export your publication as a PDF slideshow with a few clicks.

On the **File** menu, select **Publish As** > **PDF Slideshow** and then, in the **Publish PDF Slideshow** dialog, update the options in the **Slideshow Defaults** section as necessary and click **OK**.

Search *Creating a PDF slideshow* in PagePlus Help for more information.

Colour schemes

 5-15 min

When designing your publications, one of the most important factors to consider is colour. It sets the mood, sends a message and gets attention. In this tutorial, we'll introduce you to PagePlus colour schemes.

In the first section of this tutorial, we'll apply scheme colours to individual elements on a page. We'll then show you how you can edit and modify scheme colours.

By the end of this tutorial you will be able to:

* Apply a preset colour scheme.

* Apply schemed colours to objects.

* Modify an existing colour scheme.

* Save a modified scheme.

Let's begin...

1. On the **File** menu, click **Startup Assistant**.

2. On the left, click **Templates**.

3. On the **Templates** list, select **Address labels** and, from the thumbnail gallery, select the **Doodle** template.

4. Click **OK**.

    The page opens in the workspace.

Applying alternative colour schemes

Many of the elements on this page have been designed to use colour schemes. Let's look at this now by choosing a different scheme.

To apply a colour scheme:

1. At the bottom-right of the studio, click **Schemes** to display the **Schemes** tab.

You'll see an assortment of named schemes, each displaying five basic colours. The colour scheme that is currently applied is highlighted.

2. On the **Schemes** tab, click to select **Scheme 3**.

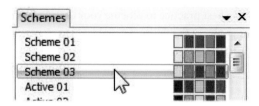

All schemed objects within the publication update with the new colours.

If you take a look at our design templates, you'll notice that these are also designed to use colour schemes so that you can change the look and feel quickly and easily.

Applying scheme colours to objects

The scheme colours work much like a paint-by-numbers system,
where various regions and elements of a page layout are coded with
numbers. In each scheme, a specific colour is assigned to each
number. You can apply a colour scheme at any point during the
design process, but it's best practice to scheme your objects from the
start. This gives you the most flexibility if you decide to change the
look and feel of a publication.

 A publication can only have one colour scheme in use at any given time.

To apply a scheme colour to an object:

1. On the **Tools** toolbar, on the ˅ **QuickShape** flyout, click
    ✿ **Quick Petal** and draw a large shape on the page.

2. On the **Swatches** tab, from the **Publications Palette** flyout, select **Scheme Colours**.

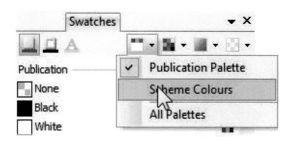

The palette displays only scheme colours.

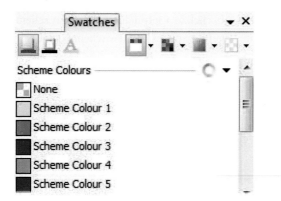

3. Ensure that the shape is selected and on the **Swatches** tab:

• Click the ⬜ **Fill** button and then click the scheme colour you want to apply to the shape's fill.

- Click the  **Line** button and apply a different scheme colour to the shape's outline.

4. On the **Schemes** tab, click to apply a different colour scheme to the publication. PagePlus applies the new scheme colours to the shape.

On the **Swatches** tab, notice that the colour scheme swatches have been replaced with the new scheme colours.

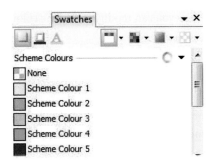

You can also apply scheme colours to text in the same way.

As you can see, when you create new elements in any publication, you can extend a colour scheme to your layout elements using the process just described.

 If you copy an object that uses scheme colours to another PagePlus publication, the object will take on the colour scheme used in the new publication.

You'll need to spend some time working out which colour combinations look best, but the mechanics of the process are simple.

 Save now! Click **File > Save As** and type a new file name.

Modifying colour schemes

If you've tried various colour schemes but haven't found one that's quite right for your publication, you can modify any of the colours in an existing scheme to create a new one.

To modify a colour scheme:

1. On the **Swatches**, on the **Scheme Colours** palette, click 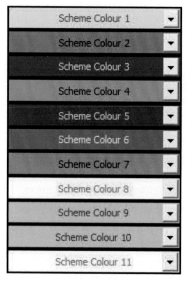 to open the **Colour Scheme Designer**.

The **Colour Scheme Designer** dialog displays the current scheme colours.

Each of the five main scheme colours (plus 6 additional colours) has its own drop-down palette, showing available colours.

2. To set or change a scheme colour, simply click the button to display the drop-down palette, and then select a new colour.

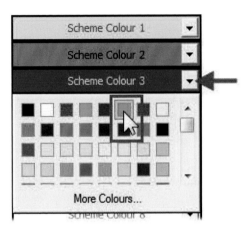

3. (Optional) If the drop-down palette doesn't contain the colour you want to use, click **More Colours** to display the **Colour Selector**.

   In the **Colour Selector** dialog, various controls allow you to choose a colour to apply or mix your own custom colours.

   - The **Colour Model** drop-down list allows you to select a colour model to choose your new colour. The **Palette** colour mode lets you modify the set of colours associated with the current publication.

   - Click **OK**.

4. When you have modified your scheme, click **OK** to apply it to your publication.

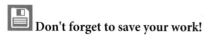 **Don't forget to save your work!**

Saving a modified scheme

When you save your publication, its current colour scheme is saved with the publication. However, if you want to use the scheme in other publications, you need to save it to the application.

To save a scheme (application):

1. On the **Tools** menu, click **Colour Scheme Designer**.

2. Select the **Colour Schemes** tab and, in the Scheme Manager pane, click **Save As**.

3. In the **New Colour Scheme** dialog, type in a new name and click **OK**.

The scheme library is updated to reflect the changes. Your new scheme will appear at the bottom of the **Scheme Manager** list.

In future, you will be able to load your saved scheme from within any project.

That's it! Now you know how to apply scheme colours to page objects and modify existing colour schemes.

There's so much more you can do!

Below is an example of what else you can do...

Update charts and tables to use colour schemes

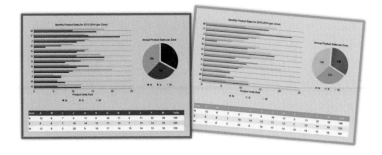

To achieve a consistent look throughout your publication, you can update your charts and tables so they use schemed colours. Chart colours can be modified as discussed in *Charts* on p. 107 and changing table formats is discussed in *Tables* on p. 93.

Object styles

15 min

The **Styles** tab contains pre-defined object styles you can quickly apply to text and objects to create dramatic effects. In this tutorial, we'll create a poster to see how simple it is to use object styles.

By the end of this tutorial you will be able to:

* Open a poster theme layout.

* Apply object styles.

* Modify object styles.

Let's begin...

1. On the **File** menu, click **Startup Assistant**.

2. On the left, click **Templates**.

3. On the **Templates** list, select **Posters** and, from the thumbnail gallery, click the **Globes** template.

4. From the **Select Colour Scheme** drop-down list, select **Scheme 3**.

5. Click **OK**.

6. In the **User Details** dialog, click **Update**.

    The page opens in the workspace.

Save now! Click **File > Save As** and type a new file name.

Using the Styles tab

The **Styles** tab contains a variety of object styles (saved attributes or properties such as line colour, fill, reflections and shadows) that can be applied with a single click.

To apply a style to an object:

1. From the **Tools** toolbar, select the ↖ **Pointer Tool**, and then click the rectangle at the top of the page.

2. On the **Styles** tab:

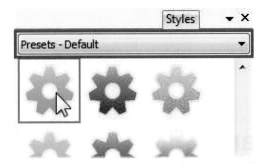

- From the category drop-down list, select **Presets - Default**.

- Click the **Default 07** thumbnail to apply it to your selected rectangle.

The Default 07 object style consists of a gradient fill, a line colour and style, and a drop shadow. These attributes are automatically applied to the rectangle.

We repeated the above steps to apply the same style to the bottom rectangle.

Object styles can just as easily be applied to text!

To apply an object style to text:

1. From the **Tools** toolbar, select the ⬉ **Pointer Tool**, and then click 'Vivamus Suspendisse'.

2. On the **Styles** tab:

    *   From the category drop-down list, select **Presets - Default**.

    *   Click the **Default 07** thumbnail to apply it to your selected text.

The Default 07 object style attributes are automatically applied to the text.

By clicking within the frame text, the object style is applied to the text only. You can, however, apply an object style to the text and surrounding text frame simultaneously. (See *Frame text* on p. 27 for more information on frame text.)

To apply a style to text and frame:

1. From the **Tools** toolbar, select the ↖ **Pointer Tool**.

2. Click 'Posuere' and then click to select the text's frame (the border turns solid).

3. On the **Styles** tab:

- From the category drop-down list, select **Presets - Default**.

- Click the **Default 26** thumbnail.

The Default 26 object style is automatically applied to the text and its frame.

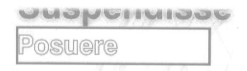

We'll quickly reposition the text and frame before moving on...

To reposition frame text:

1. With the text frame still selected, on the context toolbar, click
   ≣ **Centre-align Paragraph**.

2. Drag the text frame, using the move button, downwards so
   it sits neatly between the title above and the paragraph text
   below.

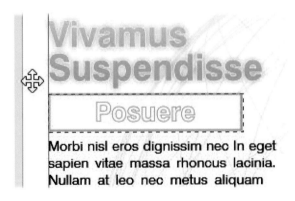

You don't have to feel restricted to applying just one object style.
You can apply multiple object styles to a single object.

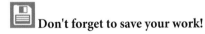 **Don't forget to save your work!**

Applying multiple styles

You can apply more than one style to an object at any point during your design process. The styles will complement rather than replace each other. This means you can 'stack up' object styles on one object to achieve your desired effect. We'll look at this now.

 When selecting an object style from the **Presets** (Default, Fun, and Materials) categories, the style may replace attributes already applied to the object. This is because the Presets category styles are designed using a variety of attributes. Furthermore, the **3D** category styles do not support some other attributes.

To apply multiple styles:

1. From the **Tools** toolbar, select the ↖ **Pointer Tool**, and then click the globe picture.

2. On the **Styles** tab:

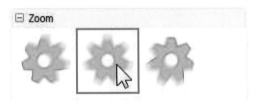

*   From the category drop-down list, select **Blurs**.

*   Click the **Zoom 02** thumbnail.

    The picture becomes blurred.

3. Again, on the **Styles** tab:

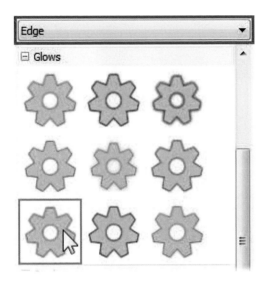

- From the category drop-down list, select **Edge**.

- Click the **Glow 06** thumbnail.

The edge style is added to the object, complementing the blur style previously applied.

Our poster design is almost complete! However, the title has now become a little lost among the glowing edge of the globe picture. We can correct this by modifying the object style applied to the title text.

 Don't forget to save your work!

Modifying object styles

When you modify an object style, any object in your publication sharing that style will update accordingly. This is a quick way to change the design of your publication and maintain consistency.

To modify object styles:

1. On the **Styles** tab:

    -   From the category drop-down list, select **Presets - Default**.

    -   Right-click the **Default 07** thumbnail and select **Edit**.

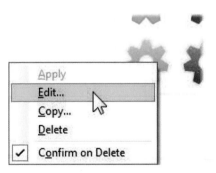

2. In the **Style Attributes Editor** dialog, double-click **Enabled** next to the **Filter Effects > Drop Shadow** option.

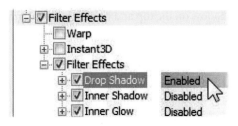

3. In the **Filter Effects** dialog, increase the **Opacity** to **80**.

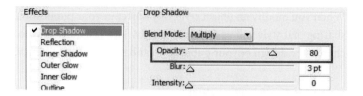

4. Click **OK** twice to exit both dialogs.

The shadow on the title text has become darker.

You will see that the shadow on the top and bottom rectangles have also darkened because they share the same style as the title text!

That's it! You now know how to use object styles to enhance your designs and how to modify object styles to suit your specific needs. Search *Using object styles* in PagePlus Help for more information.

Projects

PagePlus is perfect for completing a range of publishing projects. In this chapter we will guide you through some advanced design techniques to help you increase your project's efficiency and add polish to your publications.

2

Page numbering

 15 min

In this tutorial, we'll show you a useful way to combine master pages and page numbering. We'll also take a look at facing pages and dual master pages, so you can set up numbering based on left (verso) and right (recto) pages.

By the end of this tutorial you will be able to:

• Add page numbers to a master page.

• Use dual master pages.

• Remove a page number from a specific page.

Let's begin...

1. On the **File** menu, click **Startup Assistant**.

2. On the left, click **Templates**.

3. On the **Templates** list, select **Brochures** and, from the thumbnail gallery, click the **Vintage** template.

4. Click **OK**.

5. In the **User Details** dialog, click **Update**.

    The publication opens in the workspace.

Adding page numbers

We can easily add page numbers to every page by simply adding them to the master page(s) of our publication. PagePlus does the rest! For more information on using master pages, see *Master pages* on p. 77.

To add a page number to a master page:

1. On the **Pages** tab, click **Master Pages** to show the Master Pages pane.

    The publication currently has one master page which is applied to all pages.

2. Double-click 'MasterA' page thumbnail to display the page in the workspace.

3. On the **Tools** toolbar, click  **Standard Text Frame**.

4. Position the cursor at the bottom left of the page—two blue intersecting margin guides will appear.

5. Drag across and down the page until the blue margin guide appears on the right of the page.

   When you release the mouse button you'll see a flashing text-insertion cursor.

6. On the **Insert** menu, click **Information > Page Number**.

   The automatic page number is inserted.

The actual number will correctly update when viewed on a page (and not the master page).

7. On the context toolbar, click ≡ **Centre-align Paragraph**.

Using centred alignment on your text means that as your page number extends from 1 to 2 to 3 characters, the entire number will remain centred.

8. On the **Pages** tab, click each of the page thumbnails to display them in the workspace.

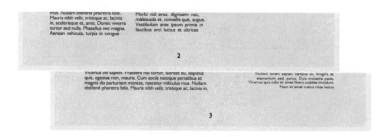

As you can see, the page number is displayed in the same place at the bottom of each page, with the exceptions of the first and last pages. This is because the first and last pages have blue rectangles on the page which mask the number—this works well for this publication as you rarely see page numbers on front and back covers!

 Save now! Click **File** > **Save As** and type a new file name.

Dual master pages

You'll frequently see brochures, magazines, and books with page numbers which alternate between the left and right side of the page, depending on which page they are on. This can be set up in PagePlus using facing pages and dual master pages.

If we set up facing pages immediately, a dual master page will be created with a blank area on the right side.

We would then have to copy the content from the left side to the right and line it up correctly.

Instead, we'll add a second, identical master page and then create facing pages. This will merge the two master pages together.

To create an additional master page:

1. On the **Pages** tab, on the Master Pages pane, double-click the 'MasterA' page thumbnail to display the page in the workspace.

2. On the Master Pages pane, click 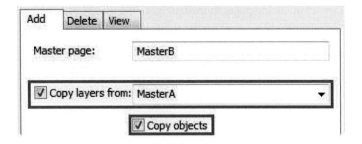 **Master Page Manager**.

3. In the **Master Page Manager** dialog:

- Select the **Add** tab.

- Select the **Copy layers from** option and select 'MasterA' from the drop-down list.

- Ensure **Copy objects** is selected.

- Click **OK**.

The publication will now contain two master pages, which are displayed in the Pages tab.

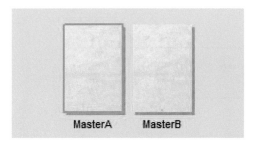

Now let's look at setting up some facing pages...

 Don't forget to save your work!

To set up facing pages:

1. On the **File** menu, select **Publication Setup**.

2. In the **Publication Setup** dialog, at the bottom of the Paper section, select the **Facing pages** option.

    The **Dual master pages** option will become available and will be selected by default.

3. Click **OK**.

The Pages tab updates to display facing pages side-by-side in both the Pages and Master Pages window. The original 'MasterA' and 'MasterB' master pages are merged.

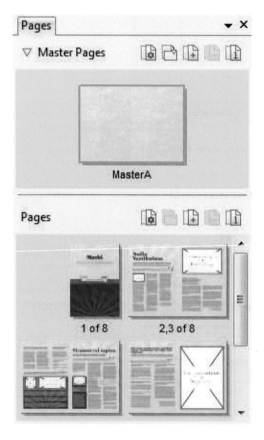

In the workspace your pages also display as a double-page spread.

Don't forget to save your work!

Now we have facing pages and dual master pages, we can set up page numbering to alternate between left and right (verso and recto) pages.

To set up dual master pages:

1. Ensure 'MasterA' is displayed in the workspace (if not, double-click 'MasterA' thumbnail on the Master Pages pane of the **Pages** tab).

2. Click to select the text frame on the left page and, on the context toolbar, select ≡ **Left-align Paragraph**.

3. Click to select the text frame on the right page and, on the context toolbar, select ≡ **Right-align Paragraph**.

4. On the **Pages** tab, double-click the **2,3 of 8** page thumbnail to display the facing pages in the workspace.

The pages now display alternating left to right page numbering.

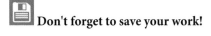 **Don't forget to save your work!**

Removing page numbers from a single page

There may be times when you want a specific page to have a master page's design but not the page number—e.g., on the seventh page there is just a single picture frame and the page number looks out of place.

We added a picture to the empty picture frame in the example above. For more information, see *Pictures* on p. 13.

We can remove the page number by promoting it from master page and then deleting it. We'll show you this next.

To promote and delete an object from a master page:

1. In the **Pages** tab, double-click the **6,7 of 8** page thumbnail.

    The double-page spread is displayed in the workspace.

2. Click to select the text frame at the bottom of the right page.

    An object toolbar will appear on the text frame showing it is located on the master page.

3. Click ⏶A **Promote from Master Page**.

    The text frame will become detached from the master page for this page only. This is shown by the updated object toolbar.

    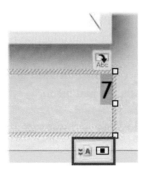

4. Click to select the text frame and then press the **Delete** key.

The page number is removed from this page but every other page remains unaffected.

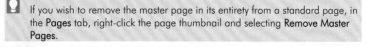

If you wish to remove the master page in its entirety from a standard page, in the **Pages** tab, right-click the page thumbnail and selecting **Remove Master Pages**.

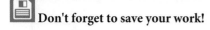 **Don't forget to save your work!**

That's it! You have successfully added page numbers to this publication. Why not have a go with your own publications? Have fun!

There's so much more you can do!

Special and mixed page number formats

In larger publications, it's common to see different styles of page numbers for different sections. For example, the introduction pages may have roman numerals while the main publication will have an Arabic (standard) format. This can be set up using the **Page Number Format** dialog available from the **Format** menu.

Search *Using page numbering* in PagePlus Help for more information.

Create event tickets

Now that you know how to format page numbers, why not combine this with a 'small publication' and automatically create sequentially numbered tickets? You could easily create individually numbered tickets for fund raisers, music gigs, club and sports events, and more.

The possibilities are endless! Here is an example that is designed to be printed on standard business card paper to get you started.

The entire ticket design is done on the master page of the **Wide Business Card** new publication type. When your design is complete, simply insert the number of pages that you wish to print so that the 'ticket' numbers increase automatically.

- We created an artistic text object and inserted a page number (**Insert > Information > Page Number**) to create the ticket number (A).

In the **Page Number Format** dialog (available from the **Format** menu), we set **Pad to 4 digits** (see note).

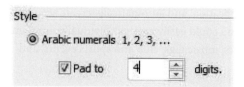

- To create the ticket stub number (B), we replicated the previous ticket number (A), and then rotated the frame by 90°.

You can prefix your automatic numbering with leading zeros using the **Page Number Format** option.

• In the **Page Number Format** dialog, select the **Pad to** option and enter the number of digits you want the number to be. (For example, for numbers between 1 and 9999, pad to 4 digits.)

• Click **OK**. All page numbers below the set number of digits will be displayed with the correct number of leading zeros.

Text styles

15 min

A text style is a set of character and/or paragraph attributes saved as a group. When you apply a style to text, you apply the whole group of attributes in just one step. The **Text Styles** tab contains pre-defined text styles you can quickly apply to text. In this tutorial, we'll look at updating and modifying preset styles and creating new text styles.

By the end of this tutorial you will be able to:

- Update a text style to match selected text.

- Modify a text style.

- Create new text styles.

- Apply text styles.

Let's begin...

1. On the **File** menu, click **Startup Assistant**.

2. On the left, click **Templates**.

3. On the **Templates** list, select **Brochures** and, from the thumbnail gallery, click the **Doodle** template.

4. Click **OK**.

5. In the **User Details** dialog, click **Update**.

    The publication opens in the workspace.

6. On the **Hintline** toolbar, click ▶ **Next Page** once to reach **Page 2**.

 **Save now!** Click **File** > **Save As** and type a new file name.

Updating and modifying text styles

All PagePlus templates and theme layouts come with pre-designed text styles which are applied throughout the publication.

However, if a particular preset style doesn't suit your specific needs, you can change it in several ways. In addition, due to all the text within the publication having a text style applied to it, once that style has been updated, all text using that style is instantly updated.

We recommend using text styles in all your publications, whether you are starting from scratch or using a template or theme layout.

To update a text style to match a selection:

1. Triple-click anywhere on the words "Nulla quis nibh. Proin ac pede vel?". This text is set to the default **Heading** text style.

2. On the context toolbar, from the fonts drop-down list, select **Blue Ridge Heavy SF**.

3. Right-click the selected text and, in the **Text Format** menu, click **Update Text Style**.

4. In the warning dialog, click **Yes** to confirm the update to the style in the entire publication.

5. In the **Text Styles** tab, you'll see that the **Heading** style has been updated to match the text and is available to use in your publication.

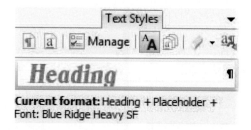

If you click through the rest of the brochure, you'll notice all Heading text has been updated to match the text style.

You can also modify a text style using the **Text Style** dialog.

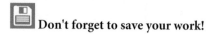 **Don't forget to save your work!**

To modify a text style:

1.   Navigate to page 2.

2.   Click on the paragraph text inside the second text frame.

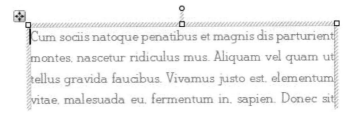

On the **Text Styles** tab, you will see that the text is assigned the
Body Text 1 paragraph style (and a Placeholder character style).

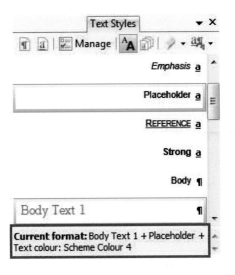

Paragraph styles are denoted by a **¶** symbol, while character styles are
denoted by a **a** symbol.

3. On the **Text Styles** tab, right-click **Body Text 1** and select **Modify Body Text 1**.

4. In the **Text Style** dialog:

- Click the **Character** category and select the **Font** sub-category.

- From the **Font** drop-down list, select **Humanst521 BT**.

- Click **OK**.

The modified style is applied to all text in the publication using Body Text 1 style.

Cum sociis natoque penatibus et magnis dis parturient montes, nascetur ridiculus mus. Aliquam vel quam ut tellus gravida faucibus. Vivamus justo est, elementum vitae, malesuada eu, fermentum in, sapien. Donec sit

Next, we'll show you how to create new text styles.

Don't forget to save your work!

Creating new text styles

Text styles can be created from scratch but, to minimize effort and maximize productivity, you can base new styles on previously created styles. This allows you to tweak a few text attributes rather than constructing the entire style.

We'll show you how to create new text styles by using a question-answer interview structure frequently seen in publications. We'll base the new styles on Body Text 1, as this style possesses most of the basic attributes we want.

To create a new Question text style:

1.   On the **Text Styles** tab, right-click **Body Text 1** and select **Base New Style on Body Text 1**.

     The **Text Style** dialog opens.

2.   Click the **General** category and in the **Name** input box, type 'Question'.

3.   Click the **Character** category and select the **Font** sub-category.

4. From the **Style** list, select **Bold (synth)** and, from the **Text fill** drop-down palette, select **Scheme Colour 2**.

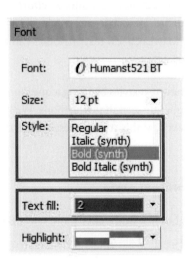

5. Click **OK**.

Your **Question** text style is added to the **Text Styles** tab.

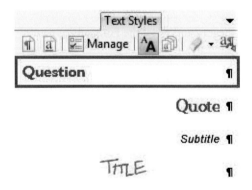

Next, we'll set up a complementary Answer style...

To create a new Answer text style:

1. On the **Text Styles** tab, right-click **Body Text 1** and select **Base New Style on Body Text 1**.

    The **Text Style** dialog opens.

2. Click the **General** category and in the **Name** input box, type 'Answer'.

3. From the **Style for following paragraph** drop-down list, select **Question**.

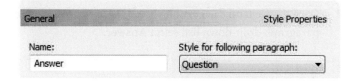

4. Click the **Character** category and select the **Font** sub-category.

5. From the **Style** list, select **Italic (synth)**.

6. Click the **Paragraph** category and select the **Alignment and Spacing** sub-category.

7. Set **After** to **10 pt**.

8. Click **OK**.

Your **Answer** text style is added to the **Text Styles** tab.

Step three ensures that when you press the **Return** key after typing the 'Answer' paragraph, the next paragraph automatically adopts the **Question** text style. This speeds up productivity!

Let's provide a similar set up for the Question style...

To modify the Question text style:

1. On the **Text Styles** tab, right-click **Question** and select **Modify Question**.

    The **Text Style** dialog opens.

2. Click the **General** category and, from the **Style for following paragraph** drop-down list, select **Answer**.

3. Click **OK**.

With our new question and answer text styles set up, let's see how they work!

 Don't forget to save your work!

Applying text styles

We'll demonstrate the question-answer interview layout with placeholder text, but feel free to write your own questions and answers. First, however, we need an empty text frame.

To delete text from a text frame:

1.   Click on the paragraph text inside the second text frame.

2.   Press **Ctrl+A** to select all the text in the frame and then press the **Delete** key.

Now for the first question...

To apply a text style:

1.   With the text frame still selected, on the **Text Styles** tab, click **Question**.

2.   Type your first question—you'll notice it is formatted as defined by the Question text style.

3.   Press the **Return** key to start a new paragraph—you'll notice on the Text Style tab that the Answer text style has been automatically selected.

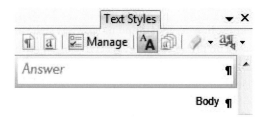

4. Type your first answer—you'll notice it is formatted as defined by the Answer text style.

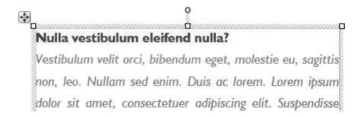

Nulla vestibulum eleifend nulla?

Vestibulum velit orci, bibendum eget, molestie eu, sagittis non, leo. Nullam sed enim. Duis ac lorem. Lorem ipsum dolor sit amet, consectetuer adipiscing elit. Suspendisse

5. Press the **Return** key to start a new paragraph—you'll notice on the Text Style tab that the Question text style has been automatically selected.

6. Repeat steps 2-5 until you have filled the text frame.

Nulla vestibulum eleifend nulla?

Vestibulum velit orci, bibendum eget, molestie eu, sagittis non, leo. Nullam sed enim. Duis ac lorem. Lorem ipsum dolor sit amet, consectetuer adipiscing elit. Suspendisse potenti.

Nullam lorem sapien, tempus ac, fringilla?

Quisque pellentesque metus ac quam. Donec magna nulla, aliquet vitae, congue ac, faucibus ut, erat. Donec sit amet neque. Donec posuere tempus massa.

That's it! You now know how to update and modify text styles and create new styles based on preset text styles. Feel free to experiment with the other preset styles within the publication. Search *Using text styles* in PagePlus Help for more information.

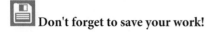 **Don't forget to save your work!**

Creating an eBook

 25-30 min

In this tutorial, we'll take you through setting up a publication in preparation for creating an eBook, which can then be published online.

The PagePlus Help topic *Publishing as eBooks* provides tips and tricks on the best ways of creating and writing a book in PagePlus, if you're planning to publish it as an eBook. These include keeping your text within text frames and using text styles. We'll look at these in more detail in this tutorial.

By the end of this tutorial you will be able to:

- Set up your publication to create the best eBook layout.

- Use text styles to create a table of contents for your eBook.

- Add hyperlinks to your eBook.

- Export your publication to an eBook format.

Let's begin...

1. On the **File** menu, click **Startup Assistant**.

2. On the left, click **New Publication**.

3. Click to select **A4** or **Letter** size paper.

    A single, blank page will open in the workspace.

Setting up your publication

WritePlus (accessible within PagePlus) provides a great environment for writing flowing text. This is perfect for publishing eBooks. Alternatively, you can work directly on the PagePlus page within text frames.

To add a text frame:

1. On the **Tools** toolbar, click **Standard Text Frame**.

2. Drag to create a text frame which fills most of the page—you can use the blue margin lines that appear to help you place your frame.

You can now type your book directly into the text frame or use WritePlus.

To use WritePlus:

1. With the text frame still selected, on the context toolbar, click  **Edit story in WritePlus**.

2. In the **WritePlus** dialog, type your book (remembering to save your work regularly).

If you have a book which is written and edited, ready for the final preparations for exporting as an eBook, you can skip straight to *Applying text styles* on p. 187.

Using the tutorial Page Content asset

If you haven't yet written your book (or wish to experiment with another book instead), we have provided a short book entitled *Self-publish Your Own eBook* to help you complete this tutorial. First, however, we'll open a new publication...

To open a new publication:

*   On the **File** menu, click **New > New Publication** (or press **Ctrl+N**).

A new publication opens based on the previously created publication (i.e. A4 or Letter size paper).

Our book, *Self-publish Your Own eBook*, can be found in the **Tutorials** assets pack.

To add tutorial assets to the Assets tab:

1. On the **Assets** tab, click  **Browse** to open the **Asset Browser**.

2. In the **Pack Files** section, select the **Tutorials** pack.

3. In the **Page Content** category, click the text frame.

4. Click **Close** to exit.

The asset is added to the Page Content category in the Asset tab.

To add page content to the page:

1. On the **Assets** tab, the **Page Content** category should be displayed (if not, click the **Page Content** header).

2. Drag the page content asset to the page.

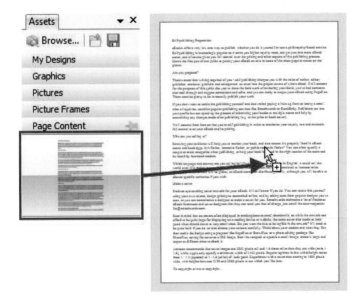

The Page Content asset consists of a single text frame containing our book.

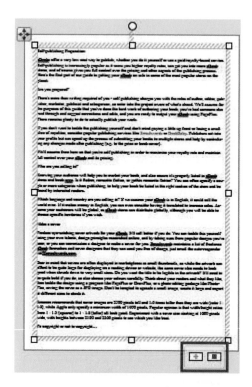

There is too much content for just a single frame, as indicated by the buttons at the bottom of the frame. So we need to create some more text frames to accommodate the book's text. We can do this using **AutoFlow**.

To autoflow text:

1. With the text frame still selected, click AutoFlow.

2. If the **Select Autoflow Frame Attributes** dialog displays, select either option and click **OK**.

PagePlus automatically creates new text frames on new pages within your publication to accommodate the entire book.

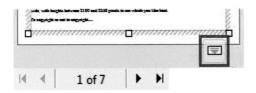

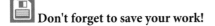

You will notice the frame's button has changed to indicate there is more text which flows into additional text frames. There are also more pages in the publication (see the **Hintline** toolbar).

Now we'll set up this book ready for exporting as an eBook.

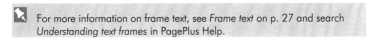

For more information on frame text, see *Frame text* on p. 27 and search *Understanding text frames* in PagePlus Help.

Don't forget to save your work!

Applying text styles

The hierarchy inherent in text styles allows PagePlus to easily build an eBook. This is one of the reasons we strongly recommend you use them in your publications. By applying particular paragraph styles to particular areas of your text, PagePlus can use these as markers within your eBook to allow readers to easily navigate it.

We will use the pre-designed text styles which come with PagePlus. These are available within all new publications. In particular, we'll concentrate on Heading 1, Heading 2, and Heading 3, to establish a hierarchical structure within our book. This will also help PagePlus build a useful table of contents for the eBook.

First we'll establish the beginning of a chapter by using Heading 1.

To apply a Heading 1 style:

1. With the text frame selected, drag to select the first sentence, 'Self-publishing Preparation'.

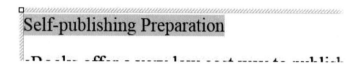

2. On the **Text Styles** tab, click **Heading 1**.

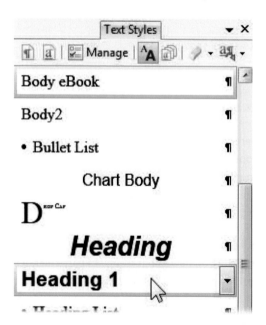

The text updates to adopt the selected style.

Self-publishing Preparation

eRooks offer a very low cost way to publish

Next, we'll establish paragraph titles as the next step down in the hierarchy by setting them to Heading 2.

To apply a Heading 2 style:

1. With the text frame selected, drag to select 'Are you prepared?'.

Are you prepared?

There's more than writing required of you -

2. On the **Text Styles** tab, click **Heading 2**.

Are you prepared?

There's more than writing required of you -

The text updates to adopt the selected style.

Heading 2 style will display in the Text Styles tab automatically once Heading 1 style is applied to text within your publication. Heading 3 will appear once Heading 2 has been applied, and so on.

You can, however, view all available styles by clicking 📖 **Show All** on the **Text Styles** tab.

3. Apply **Heading 2** text style to 'Who are you selling to?', 'Make a cover', and 'To copyright or not to copyright...' to complete the page layout.

At your leisure, continue to apply Heading text styles throughout the publication. We recommend setting the paragraph titles 'In the USA', 'In the UK', and 'Other territories' to Heading 3 as they are important but do not warrant a Heading 2 text style because they are part of the 'Do you need an ISBN?' discussion.

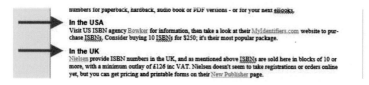

We'd also recommend setting 'Publishing your eBook', 'Publishing on Amazon', and 'References' as Heading 1 to begin new chapters.

Next we'll explore one main feature about eBooks—the ability to include cross-referencing hyperlinks!

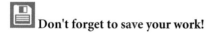 **Don't forget to save your work!**

Adding hyperlinks

Hyperlinks are a great way of directing readers to a website which can provide them with more information on the topics discussed in your book or to connect them directly with any referenced material within your book.

Although you can place hyperlinks in your book, not all eBook readers support them. The hyperlinked text will still display but may not redirect to the hyperlinked content. If you have hyperlinked text within your book, you may wish to create a 'References' chapter at the end of your book which provides hyperlink details. See our References section at the end of the tutorial book.

To add hyperlinks to text:

1. On the **Hintline** toolbar, click ▸ **Next Page** several times to reach **Page 6**.

2. Click to select the text frame and then drag to select 'getting published' in the **Conclusion** section.

3. On the **Standard** toolbar, click 🔗 **Hyperlink**.

4. In the **Hyperlinks** dialog:

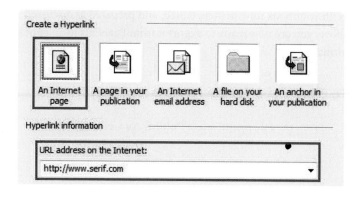

*   Select **An Internet page**.

*   In the **URL address on the Internet** input box, type a web address (e.g. http://www.serif.com).

- Click **OK**.

The text will update to a hyperlink format (underlined and shaded) and will also display a hyperlink button when selected.

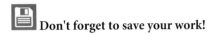

Now we've finished preparing our publication, it's finally time to export it as an eBook!

Don't forget to save your work!

Publishing an eBook

With your book now written, edited, and prepared as discussed above, you are now ready to export it from PagePlus to an eBook format.

To export your publication as an eBook:

- From the **File** menu, select **Publish As > eBook**.

  The **Publish as eBook** dialog will open.

The **Publish as eBook** dialog is so important in getting your eBook right, we're going to step through it carefully...

To set Document Info settings:

1. In the **Title** input box, type the title of your book (in our case, 'Self-publish Your Own eBook').

2. Fill in the remaining fields (Author, Subject, Publisher, etc,.) as appropriate.

3. In the **ID** field, a **UUID** has already been generated for you—to generate another UUID, click **Generate**.

- or -

From the **ID** drop-down list, select **ISBN** and type in your book's ISBN (if required).

- or -

If you have an Amazon ID (ASIN), select **Custom** from the drop-down list and type in your book's ASIN.

4. To add a cover to your eBook, click **Browse**, navigate to your image file and click **Open**.

If you're interested in creating an eBook which can be viewed on a Kindle (or Kindle application), you will need to export your eBook as a *.mobi file. Alternatively, you can skip this step and export your eBook directly as an *.epub file for non-Kindle devices and applications.

To create a MOBI file for Kindle:

1. Click the **Output** option on the left of the dialog.

2. Click **Download Kindlegen from Amazon** and follow the procedures to download the **Kindlegen.exe** file.

3. Back in PagePlus, click **Browse** and then locate **Kindlegen.exe** and click **Open**.

The next step will highlight the importance of setting text styles within your publication (see *Applying text styles* on p. 187).

 With eBooks, chapters start on a new page.

To set Styles settings:

1. Click the **Styles** option on the left of the dialog.

2. Click **Heading 1** then:

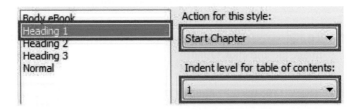

•   Set the **Action for this style** as **Start Chapter**.

This will ensure all Heading 1 style text starts a new chapter.

•   Set the **Indent level for table of contents** as **1**.

This will ensure Heading 1 style text appears to the farthest left on the table of contents.

3. Click **Heading 2** then:

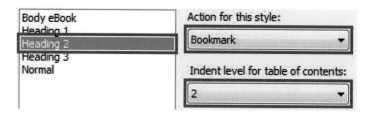

•   Set the **Action for this style** as **Bookmark**.

This will ensure all Heading 2 style text appears in the table of contents.

•   Set the **Indent level for table of contents** as **2**.

This will ensure Heading 2 style text appears indented from the chapter titles in the table of contents.

Now to finish the exporting of your publication to an eBook!

To complete your eBook creation:

1. In the **Publish as eBook** dialog, click **OK**.

2. In the **Publish eBook** dialog:

- Navigate to your chosen location.

- Type in a **File name** for your eBook.

- (Optional) From the **Save as type** drop-down list, select **Kindle files (*.mobi)**.

  This option is only available if you followed the *To create a MOBI file for Kindle* procedure on p. 194.

- Click **Save**.

If there are any problems with your eBook, in PagePlus the **Preflight** tab will open displaying all the issues. If you added hyperlinks to your publication, these will be highlighted in the tab.

For more information about the Preflight tab and resolving issues, search *eBook publishing warnings* in PagePlus Help.

PagePlus will export your publication as an eBook and it will automatically open in your default eBook PC reader application.

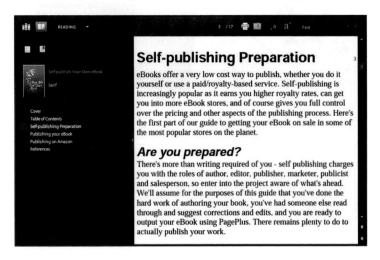

That's it! You have now created an eBook ready for sharing with the world.

The next stage of the eBook publishing process is to submit your eBook to Amazon and other online stores. Start by visiting the *Kindle Direct Publishing* portal (https://kdp.amazon.com) and reading the guidelines. Other online stores will have similar steps that you can follow. More information on publishing your eBook is available from our Page Content publication, *Self-publish Your Own eBook*, available in the installed **Tutorials** assets pack.

 There are a variety of devices which allow you to preview your kindle book (*.mobi) on your computer, however, if you install Kindle Previewer software (available from Amazon Kindle publishing), you can also use this as a way to validate the content formatting of your book to ensure it will display correctly on the entire range of Kindle devices and applications.

Why not create an eBook front cover in PagePlus?

1. Simply open a new publication (**File > New > New Publication**).

2. To work in pixels rather than centimetres, click **Tools > Options** and then select **Pixels** from the **Units** drop-down list from the **Layout > Rulers** section.

3. On the **File** menu, select **Publication Setup** and then, using the **Width** and **Height** settings, adjust the publication size.

> Experiment with a cover size starting at 800 pixels wide, with heights between 1050 and 1280 pixels to see which you like best.

4. Design your cover on the page using artistic text, pictures and assets (see p. 3, 13, and 45, respectively).

5. Export your page as a picture (**File > Export as Picture**), ensuring the **Export Area** is set to **Page**—for more information, search *Exporting as a picture* in PagePlus Help.

> Exporting your eBook as a *.mobi (for Kindle)? You can design your cover on the first page of your publication—it will automatically become your eBook cover. Design using floating objects (not placed in a text frame) to prevent them appearing within the body of the eBook. This method of cover design will display errors during preflight. Search *Preflight check* and *eBook publishing warnings* in PagePlus Help for more information.

Creative Showcase

PagePlus X7 provides many professionally designed **Pro Template Pack** and **Theme Layout** publications to help you get started easily. Furthermore, PagePlus includes a range of assets which can be used to quickly build up content and preset object styles which can applied to any page objects for instant results.

3

Pro Templates

PagePlus provides a selection of **Pro Template Pack** publications
that are populated with pictures and text placeholders which you
can start using straight away.

To open a Pro Template Pack publication:

1. On the **File** menu, click **Startup Assistant**.

2. On the left, click **Templates**.

3. On the **Templates** list, select **Pro Template Packs**, and from the
    thumbnail gallery, click to select a publication from one of the
    PagePlus X7 Pro Templates.

4. Click **OK**.

We'll showcase the **Clearfield Beach House** (as selected above),
Olivia Lenton Studio and **Villereccio Pizzeria** templates next.

 You can get more **Pro Template Packs** from Serif's template store. Visit
http://www.serif.com/templates

Clearfield Beach House

Olivia Lenton Studio

Villereccio Pizzeria

Theme Layouts

PagePlus provides a selection of **Theme Layout** templates with picture and text placeholders that you can use as starting points for your own publications. They are categorized into **Editorial**, **Graphical**, **Illustrative**, and **Textured**.

To open a theme layout publication:

1. On the **File** menu, click **Startup Assistant**.

2. On the left, click **Templates**.

3. On the **Templates** list, select **Theme Layouts**, and from the thumbnail gallery, click to select a publication from one of the Theme Layout templates.

4. (Optional) For multi-page publications, select your pages.

5. Click **OK**.

We'll showcase the **Ecrue** (as selected above), **Heirloom** and **Rugged** templates next.

Ecrue

Heirloom

Rugged

Assets and object styles

PagePlus comes installed with a range of assets which you can quickly add to a publication to build up content and pre-designed object styles which can be applied to page objects to create some fantastic effects.

Assets

PagePlus assets, available from the **Assets Browser** and **Assets** tab, range from individual objects to full page designs. Assets are organized into the following categories: **Graphics**, **Pictures**, **Picture Frames**, **Page Content**, **Backgrounds** and **Pages**. Many of the assets are associated with PagePlus's **Theme Layouts** but are designed to be used with any publication you are working on.

For more information on using assets within your publications, see the dedicated tutorial, *Assets*, on p. 45.

We'll showcase the **Graphics - Stack**, **Page Content - Elements** and **Pages - Industrial** assets next.

Object styles

The **Styles** tab provides you with pre-designed object styles which you can apply to any object on your page.

For more information on using object styles within your publications, see the dedicated tutorial, *Object styles*, on p. 141.

We'll showcase the **Preset - Defaults** and **Charts** categories on p. 213 and 214, respectively.

Graphics - Stack

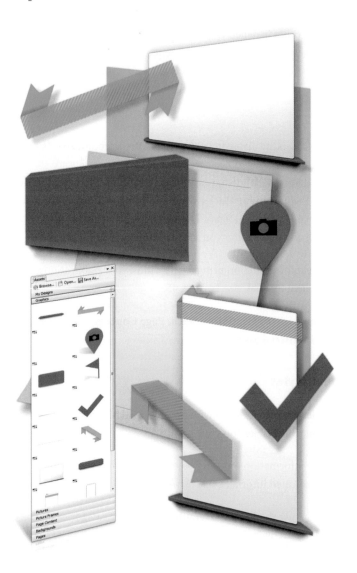

Page Content - Elements

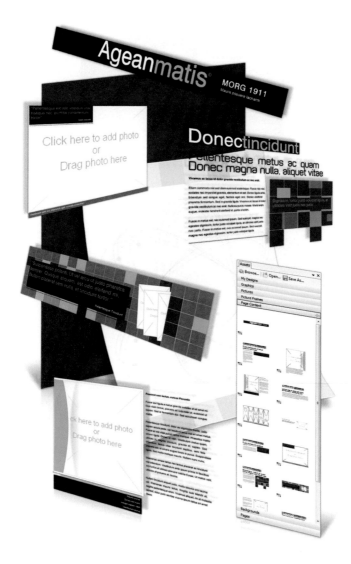

Pages - Industrial

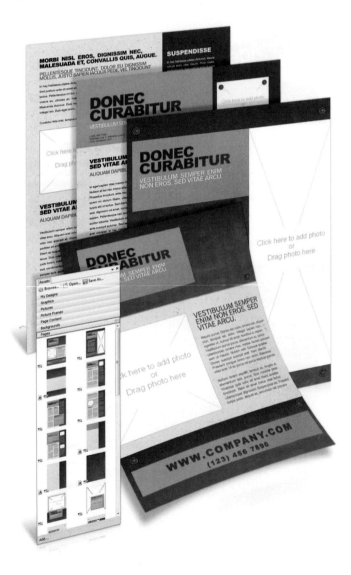

Preset - Defaults

Charts

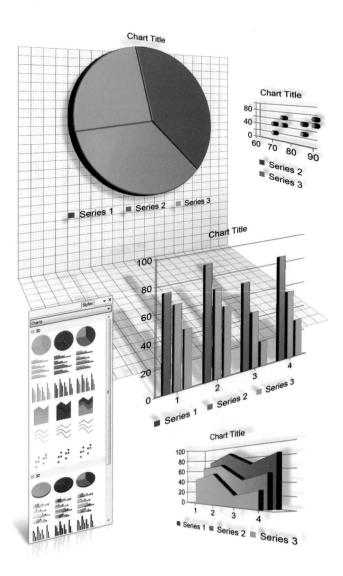